Within you is a spirit that lived before your physical birth and that will continue to live after your physical death. Eternity goes both ways. You lived—not as another person but as yourself—in a spiritual pre-life.

God had clear and beautiful purpose in providing you with this mortal phase of eternity. Part of that purpose has to do with the struggle of being on your own here, without memory of there.

But you do have some sliver of memory —just enough to feel it is true when you hear it—just enough to believe in the earlier life of your own soul.

ALSO BY RICHARD EYRE

The Discovery of Joy
Spiritual Serendipity
Stewardship of the Heart
*Lifebalance**
The Awakening (a novel)
What Manner of Man
*Teaching Your Children Values**
Don't Just Do Something, Sit There
*3 Steps to a Strong Family**
*Teaching Your Children Responsibility**
*How to Talk to Your Child about Sex**
*Teaching Your Children Sensitivity**
*Teaching Your Children Joy**
The Wrappings and the Gifts
*Children's Stories to Teach Joy**
*Alexander's Amazing Adventures: Values for Children***
Simplified Husbandship/Simplified Fathership
Free to Be Free
The Secret of the Sabbath
* Coauthored with Linda J. Eyre
**Audiotape series

Life
Before
Life

Origins of the soul . . .
knowing where you came from
and who you really are

營 營 營 營 營

New York Times #1 Bestselling Author

RICHARD EYRE

**SHADOW
MOUNTAIN**

Page 25: "Little Gidding" from *Four Quartets*, ©1942 by T. S. Eliot and renewed 1970 by Esme Valerie Eliot, reprinted by permission of Harcourt, Inc.

Visit us at www.shadowmountain.com

Library of Congress Cataloging-in-Publication Data

Eyre, Richard M.

    Life before life: origins of the soul . . . knowing where you came from and who you really are / Richard M. Eyre

      p.   cm.
    ISBN 1-57345-782-5
    1. Pre-existence. I. Title.

BX8643.P67 E97 2000
233—dc21   00-033887

Printed in the United States of America   72082-6673

10 9 8 7 6 5 4 3 2

Contents

Preface: Trailing Clouds of Glory   vii

1   Questions of Eternity   1
Believing in the future / Believing in the past
(two names for the same spiritual quest)

2   Our Spiritual Sense   17
What most people already believe (to some degree)

3   Our Spiritual Compass   51
Why people know what they know (and how)

Intermission: Kilimanjaro and Kolob   67
Deciding to write about life before life

4   Our Spiritual Past   93
What most people don't yet know (but can)

5   Answers for Mortality   119
Why it helps to know (what changes when we do)

6   Conscious Application   153
Using the insight to change your life (and your world)

Postscript: Continuing the Quest   175

Reading Group Guide   177

Acknowledgments

Thanks to my wife and eternal partner, Linda, who encouraged me on this book despite its potential for the kind of controversial exposure she dislikes . . . and to my father, Dean Eyre, who I believe helped me from the other side.

Thanks also to Sheri Dew, Don Gull, and Emily Watts, my team at Shadow Mountain. They believed in the importance of the subject, they never said okay until something was okay, and they became my friends.

Preface: Trailing Clouds of Glory

Our birth is but a sleep and a forgetting:
The soul that rises with us, our life's Star,
Hath had elsewhere its setting,
And cometh from afar:
Not in entire forgetfulness,
And not in utter nakedness,
But trailing clouds of glory do we come
From God, who is our home.

Heaven lies about us in our infancy . . .

William Wordsworth
Ode: Intimations of Immortality

Books about life *after* life are generally written by those who claim to have experienced it, albeit briefly. Life *before* life, on the other hand, if it exists at all, has been experienced by us all. A book about it should be written by one who, through prayer and other process, has found insights that ring true and spiritual memory that is partially reopened.

I'm not sure why I've had this experience—of the sliver of

slightly reopened spiritual memory—unless it is so I can write it and share it. Nor do I know whether to call what I've experienced "impressions" or "visions" or simply "answers." They range from reading something and knowing it's true . . . to holding a newborn child, staring into his eyes, and feeling that he has just come from somewhere else . . . to actual spiritual glimpses of our former spiritual home or of spirits who still live there awaiting their turn to come to earth.

Some of my experience may not be too far removed from yours. Wordsworth's poem says our souls came from God "trailing clouds of glory . . . not in entire forgetfulness, and not in utter nakedness." The spark of divine nature that glows or smolders within each of us occasionally prompts a feeling, a longing, almost a spiritual homesickness for a higher sphere, a sudden stab of sweet sentiment that seems to transcend where we are now and open the briefest glimpse of where we once were. It is as though the veil of forgetfulness were a semi-permeable membrane, blocking conscious memory but letting certain feelings seep through.

It is these feelings, these "trailing clouds of glory," that I am counting on to allow you to believe what I have written in this book. Things that are real carry with them a ring of truth that is recognizable to our spirits—spirits that, I believe, with Wordsworth, come "from afar . . . from God, who is our home."

Parts of this book are very personal. I can't tell you what I believe about the soul without telling you something of how I came to believe it. Some of the "personal parts" will reveal that I think of myself as a spiritual and religious person, that I belong to a Christian church that teaches of a life before life, and that I believe deeply in prayer and in the inspiration and guidance that prayer can bring. Still, I've drawn from a diverse array of sources and tried not to overemphasize my particular religious persuasions because this book is not about individual differences, religious or otherwise. It is about the most fundamental spiritual similarity of all—that we are all eternal souls who came here from a premortal place, from a life before life. This insight, this belief, can come to anyone and to everyone, to people who belong to any religion and to people who belong to no religion. It is a truth that is buried deep within us and that carries with it its own conviction, a conviction that can enter the soul of anyone who will ponder and pray. Belief comes through the feelings of our individual spirits. When we encounter some concept that carries light, it feels familiar to the very spirits within us that came from before.

Most readers who know me at all know me as a writer of parenting and family books. Why, they might wonder, have I jumped out of that genre? Perhaps I haven't. You may agree as you read that this is the ultimate family and parenting book. In our life before life we lived as spirits and as part of the spiritual family of God, His sons and daughters. As our true and eternal parent, He provided a plan for our progression that involved a mortal experience on a physical earth. Knowing this can make us better children, better siblings, better parents, and better people.

The question of where our souls originated has intrigued if not obsessed me since childhood, partly because of the sense that its answer would so enlighten the other two eternal questions of why we're here and where we're going. So perhaps I've asked it harder and longer than most. And maybe the ever-present question became a frame within which I could see answers that others miss.

Whatever the reasons or the process, the spiritual past has opened itself to me enough that I dare write of it. The openings have come sometimes as I read and feel the words of those I revere, from the verse of poets to the scripture of prophets; sometimes in solitary answers to meditation or prayer; and sometimes completely unexpectedly, out of the blue, when some beautiful or perfect moment touches or moves something deep inside. Some of these openings felt almost like dreams. But whereas dreams seem less real and less logical as we think of them after we're awake, these openings seem more and more real.

As I attempt to write about these openings, help me by reading about them with an open heart. It is difficult to write in words that which comes in feelings. But I believe if both of us try, my spirit can code feelings into words as I write, and your spirit can encode them back into feelings as you read.

Richard Eyre

Kolob Canyon

1

Questions
of Eternity

❧ ❧ ❧ ❧ ❧

Believing in the future / Believing in the past
(two names for the same spiritual quest)

"From God, Who Is Our Home"

Let me begin with an experience that I hope will share some insight as to why I chose to write on this subject and that will set a personal context for some questions about our origin and our eternal souls.

We were living in England during a particularly busy and challenging time of our lives. Both my wife, Linda, and I were involved in projects that required extensive travel and that were taxing emotionally as well as physically. We were desperately trying to juggle the demands of our work with the needs of our children and family. The last thing that would have occurred to us at that juncture was having another child.

Yet it did occur to us. It kept occurring to both of us that we should try to become pregnant again and add a child to our family. At first I tried to ignore it; Linda did too. It was just incongruous with reality. It didn't fit with where we were in our lives. I couldn't imagine where the feeling was coming from. Certainly not from within me—there was nothing logical or practical about it, no one had suggested it, we didn't even know anyone else who was pregnant or who would put the thought into our minds. But the thought that we should have another baby—*now*—wouldn't go away, and the thought felt like it was coming from outside of us, from some intelligence or presence that was not our own. It troubled Linda even more than it did me. The thought of a new baby on top of everything else she was dealing with right then simply overwhelmed her.

We had asked God for each of our other children, prayed and asked that we could conceive when it seemed that the timing and the situation were right. This time we found ourselves doing just the opposite, essentially explaining to God that the timing and situation were wrong and asking Him to remove this feeling, or at least to allow us to conclude that it was nonsense. When that didn't happen, we felt we had to become more open and more sincere in our prayers, trying to summon our faith and to ask God to let us know His will. We decided to set aside some time one Sunday afternoon to focus on the issue and to pray together for an answer.

The answer that came was unexpected and remarkable. It completely removed our anxiety and replaced it with calm. There was light and clarity within that calm, and we understood that the promptings we had been feeling came from God.

Within the answer to that singular prayer, God told us, through an unmistakable feeling deep within our souls, that there was an existing spirit in a spiritual place awaiting entry into mortality and into our family, and that the entry should happen now. Furthermore, He told us *about* that spirit—that he was a spirit of remarkable peace and calm, that he would be an easy baby, that the nature of his comfortable and serene spirit would actually ease our burdens rather than increase them and would draw our family (and our priorities) closer as we came together to care for and love this new child.

I'll never forget the feeling as we concluded that prayer—nor will Linda. We had knelt down feeling troubled, concerned, confused about a prompting that we couldn't understand or accept. We got up feeling completely at peace, reassured as to what to do, and certain in our souls that there was a spiritual place and that in that spiritual place was a particular, unique person who was preparing to join us, a person whose nature we already knew.

There is a brief postscript to this story about still another level of assurance we received that Sunday afternoon. We had asked our eldest child, Saren, who was seven, to play with her younger brother and sister upstairs so Linda and I could be alone for our prayer. She wanted to know what we were praying about, so we simplified, "About whether to have another baby." After our prayer and within the peaceful aura of our answer, we called up the stairs for Saren to come down so we could thank her—she'd kept everything relatively quiet for nearly two hours. She came down with a twinkle in her eye and three pieces of paper in her hand and a grinning little brother and sister behind her. "We prayed too," she said, "and we marked our votes on these papers." She handed me three homemade ballots, each with two crayon-drawn squares, one labeled "Yes" and one "No." Each of them had an "X" in the yes box.

The longer-range postscript is that our son Talmadge joined our family ten months later and was (and is) all that God had promised us he would be.

A Two-Way Eternity

Polls show that more than 95 percent of Americans (and the figure is similar in most other parts of the world) profess a belief in God or some higher power, and that between 70 and 80 percent (depending on how the question is phrased) believe there is a spirit or soul in human beings that continues to live after the physical death of the body (see George Gallup and D. Michael Lindsay, *Surveying the Religious Landscape*, Morehouse Publishing, 1999).

Where did that soul in which most of us believe come from? If we are spiritual beings, where did our spirits originate? Did they flare into existence at the moment we were physically conceived or born? Or did they have a spiritual beginning and come from a spiritual place?

Many conclude that a spirit that goes on beyond death must have had a beginning that predates birth. To some, this suggests reincarnation—a soul that recycles through different bodies and different lives, even perhaps through different species. Others are repelled by this idea, feeling that they have always been who they are but that they may have come from some other place, "not in entire forgetfulness," as Wordsworth wrote.

Most of us, at times, have glimpses of almost-memory, fleeting sensations that there is more to us than our few years here on earth, feelings of haunting familiarity with things or people we have just encountered. Some call these feelings déjà vu, and many wonder if they are evidence of life before life.

The more one ponders, the more the idea of a one-way eternity (or a spiritual existence extending into the future but not into the past) seems illogical. If there is a spirit within us, it makes sense to suppose that it came from a spiritual place. It is that spiritual place, that "premortal" or "prephysical" existence, that this book is about.

We all want to know of life *after* life because it increases our faith. Knowing of life *before* life can do the same, perhaps even more so. If one writes of a near-death experience and a place beyond, we are reading about what happened to *him*. If another tells us about experiences before birth, we are reading about what happened to each of *us*. If we believe that we came from another place, and from God, everything expands—from our perspective to our own self-worth. We begin to see purpose and meaning in life's experience, and our hope in life hereafter becomes balanced by our faith in life before.

Questions of Eternity

The question of life *after* life fascinates us. Some who have had near-death experiences have felt their spirits leave their bodies and move toward a better, brighter place. Some of those have written books about this beginning of afterlife, and the books have become bestsellers.

Little wonder that we have intense curiosity about after-life—we're all headed for it. And accounts of people who at least started to experience it can bolster our hope and our faith.

"What happens to us after we die?" "Why are we here?" These are perhaps the two most asked, most pondered, most personal, most important questions ever asked (and always asked) by mankind.

Their answers (or various attempts or starts at answers) are found throughout the spiritual and the secular, in Bibles and in bestsellers, in sermons and in seminars, in scripture and in self-help.

The questions are ponderous, powerful, and personal because within them we seek a framework in which to live. But they are incomplete (and unanswerable) without a third question, which is: "Where did we come from?"

How can we grasp what and who and why we are without knowing from whence we came? Even in earth time the present and future can only be well grasped or well planned in the context of the past.

As a management consultant, I often tell that to clients. If you think only of the future, never connecting it to the past, you will repeat certain mistakes and fail to notice opportunities. Knowing your past helps you to know yourself and to understand where you can go. I use a boating analogy: The best way to keep a straight course is not to look in front of you. Instead, you look back at your wake and keep it straight. This works on a lake ... or in life ... or in eternity.

Questions of This Life

In closer focus than the three great questions of eternity are the wide array of questions we ask about this life—questions that affect our perspectives and our priorities, our faith and our future.

- ❧ Why do some things seem so familiar when we see them for the first time?
- ❧ Why are some children within the same family so completely different from each other?
- ❧ Where do our gifts, our inclinations, our talents, and our propensities come from?

❧ Why is there such difference and division among religions—would not God lead us all in one way?

❧ Why do most people feel such need, such drive, for independence, for ownership, for control?

❧ Why are we so attached to nature and to animals? Why does the beauty of the natural world appeal to us so instinctively?

❧ Why do some things (and some people) "ring true" to us and feel right, while other things feel wrong?

❧ Why are we instantly drawn to some people, almost as though we've known them forever?

❧ Why are we "moved" and "touched" by some things when we have no intention of becoming emotional?

❧ Why is there such suffering, such cruelty in the world? Could any of it serve a purpose?

❧ Why is there such inequality and apparent unfairness—some who have so much, some so little?

Only in the context of a spiritual future and a spiritual past are such questions even approachable. One phase of ongoing life establishes the needs and parameters for the next phase, and our individual freedom of choice both requires and creates the broadest diversity. Without an eternal context there are only the comfortless nonanswers of chaos and chance.

With thought and with belief, we realize that all these and a hundred other questions about ourselves and about our lives are really subquestions of the three eternal questions—whence, why, and whither. And of these three, the most fundamental, the first in sequence, and the one that brings most light to bear on the other two is *whence*.

A Third Alternative

Among the 70 to 80 percent of Americans who believe in a soul that continues to live after the body dies, nearly half believe in reincarnation—that their spirit preexisted in a different body and will continue to exist in still another body, perhaps with intervals and a final destination in heaven (Gallup and Lindsay, *Surveying the Religious Landscape*, 28, 32).

The other half seem to believe in some form of heaven as the spirit's destination but have no belief in a life before, apparently assuming that this spirit originated at their birth.

In other words, the two options, it seems, for those who believe in an eternal soul, are that our spirits either jumped from one life form to another until they got to us or they suddenly sprang into existence at the moment we were born or conceived.

Most people, I believe, are not fully comfortable with either option. Reincarnation, while it "answers" certain questions, essentially requires that we share our personalities with a lot of other people, past and present. It makes us less our own. And the notion of our spirits just flaring instantly into existence seems simplistic, shallow, and inadequate in light of all the nuances and complexities of who we each are.

There is a third alternative—the one this book asks you to consider. It is that our spirits lived long before they inherited our bodies—not in other persons but in another place, in a premortal realm where we each developed and became who we are and from where we foresaw this physical life as a continuing phase in our experience and our spiritual progression.

Hope and Worth

Why is life *after* life so much more talked and written about than life *before* life? Here are two possible answers and a counter thought to each:

1. It seems more natural and legitimate to predict, project, preview, and prognosticate the future because it hasn't happened yet. Predictions and conjecture are *about* the future. When dealing with the past, we're accustomed to having a history of remembered and recorded facts. Still, when there is no documented history of a particular period, we don't assume it didn't happen; we look for clues and insights, and we try to reconstruct it.

We should do the same for our spiritual past. To those who believe in a spirit or soul, the best assumption is that it has a past—a past we should look for and be vitally interested in. We won't find our spiritual past in dusty relics or archeological digs. We will find it deep within our own souls, unlocked and encoded only by our personal faith and prayers. And we should not expect too much detail. Our life on this earth has a purpose, part of which has to do with developing independence and faith, a process that would be undermined by a full memory of who and what and where we were before. But faith is strengthened by knowing we existed before and knowing there is a purpose in our being here.

In the spiritual sense, then, our past is very much like our future—known only through faith and predicted (or remembered) only by spiritual vision.

2. Some would say that thinking about and believing in life after life is more important and more valuable because it gives us *hope*. Yet believing in and understanding life before life can give us *worth*. Believing that we're more than a genetic coincidence, that we brought with us personalities and characters and gifts we developed in a place before, and that we are children of God sent here for a purpose . . . these beliefs can give us a self-respect and a sense of spiritual identity that can ennoble us and add dimension to our hope for a life to come.

What could be more important and more valuable than these two eternal "bookends" of hope and worth?

Our Spiritual Sense

❦ ❦ ❦ ❦ ❦

What most people already believe (to some degree)

Prompters of a Belief in the Before

Some thoughts seem new and yet old at the same time. The concept of a life before this life is new to most people . . . yet somehow familiar.

As we ponder the possibility, we feel simultaneously disturbed and comforted. The concept gives us a whole other realm to wonder and worry about. Yet there is a reassuring resonance in the notion that there is more to us than a brand-new cluster of physical cells.

It turns out that people have been wondering about (and drawing conclusions about) a preearthly existence since this present existence began. And testimonials, if not evidence, of a life before life exist all around us. Most people have experienced various parts of this evidence but have not consciously made all the connections. There are, in other words, things we know but do not quite know that we know.

This chapter shares a number of different things that most of us have either experienced or been exposed to—things ranging from personal feelings to universal conscience, from poetry and proverbs to mythology and movies—all things that point us toward a life before life. It also includes references to a premortal life from scripture, from Greek philosophy, from early Christianity, and from popular modern writers. The bottom line is that life before life is anything but a new or isolated notion. It is a belief that has existed throughout time and throughout cultures.

This chapter's references, evidences, feelings, and testimonies of a premortal life are not intended as "proofs" or "convincers," but they are reassurances that it is natural to think about and connect to one's eternal soul. They are *prompters* of belief in the before. Eighteen such prompters follow, not in any particular order of importance. They are numbered so you can mentally keep track of them and perhaps be reassured by how many there are—by how common and natural it is to believe in a life before.

1. Déjà Vu

The place just seemed so familiar to me." "I'm sure I've met you somewhere, sometime." "I swear this has happened before."

What the French call *déjà vu* comes in many forms, ranging from a faint glimmer of familiarity in a new situation or a new person to an extensive, unexplainable knowledge of something you've never learned or experienced before or a natural skill or inclination you have not intentionally developed. Sometimes there is even an apparent familiarity with things that happened hundreds of years before.

Temporal, physical thinking tries to brush it off: "Just looks like someone else." "Must have been there once and forgotten." "Probably read it in a book or saw a picture of it sometime." Yet these explanations don't seem quite adequate or accurate— especially right while the déjà vu is taking place. At the moment we actually feel it, there is a sense of distance and mystery and a feeling that we've been around longer than we know.

Déjà vu is a favorite concept of some reincarnationists, who explain it simply: "It happened to the person you were in an earlier life." But it fits equally well to one who believes in a spirit that originated elsewhere—a spirit that had experiences and met others in a preearth place and perhaps from there saw brief preview glimpses of his or her life here, or even of the life of one who would be his or her ancestor. These glimpses, which lie deep within our spirits, may be what trigger our most profound moments of déjà vu.

Almost everyone I've discussed this concept with has had a déjà vu story to tell. Typical was the incident one editor related of a woman she had just met whom she felt like she had known forever. "Everything about her and about our interaction was familiar and easy and natural," she said. "It was more like we'd just found each other rather than just met each other."

2. "PBEs"

Though not nearly as common as déjà vu, the experience of some type of contact or communication with a spirit not yet born has been documented by many people, particularly parents. Enough of these experiences have been reported in recent years that researchers have given them a name: Pre-Birth Experiences, or PBEs. The conclusion is that this type of spiritual experience has been occurring in all cultures throughout human history.

One such researcher, Harold Widdison, a Ph.D. professor of medical sociology, indicates that he has, over a twenty-five-year span, interviewed hundreds of people who have experienced PBEs or Near-Death Experiences (NDEs). Widdison says, "I am absolutely convinced that these are authentic descriptions of actual events." He compares NDEs and PBEs as follows:

"NDEs suggest the existence of a *post*-Earth life where we go *after* physical life ends. The soul crosses over from the Earth realm to a nonmaterial realm. In contrast, PBEs suggest the existence of a *pre*mortal realm where souls reside *before* they come down to Earth. In PBEs, the not-yet-born soul crosses over into this *Earth* realm from the realm of pre-Earth life and makes some form of contact with people living on Earth."

He goes on to categorize seven types of message or communication from unborn spirits: "1) The unborn soul gives a message that the time for conception is near; 2) the unborn soul shares that he or she has a special mission to accomplish on Earth; 3) a radiation of love emanates from the unborn soul; 4) gratitude is expressed by the unborn soul for bringing him or her to Earth; 5) the unborn soul predicts a significant future event that affects the mission of the unborn soul and/or the family that the unborn soul will be born into; 6) the unborn soul expresses excitement or reluctance about entering Earth life; 7) a message of warning or protection is given by the unborn soul regarding an impending danger, especially if this danger may jeopardize the unborn soul's arrival on Earth" (quoted in Eliot Jay Rosen, *Experiencing the Soul*, Hay House, 1999, 52).

An individual unfamiliarity with PBEs may have more to do with our inability to receive impressions than with the ability of unborn spirits to send them.

3. Poetry

Wordsworth is not the only one. Many poets have hinted at something more . . . something before.

Poet and lyricist Eliza R. Snow wrote of times when

> . . . *a secret something*
> *Whispered, "You're a stranger here,"*
> *And I felt that I had wandered*
> *From a more exalted sphere.*

The final stanza of T. S. Eliot's "Little Gidding" in *Four Quartets* might be interpreted as a reference to a prelife from which we were sent for further exploration, a probe for origin with Adam and Eve represented as "the children in the apple tree." In that view, Eliot even suggests *why* we don't know more about our prelife—"because not looked for."

We shall not cease from exploration
And the end of all our exploring
Will be to arrive where we started
And know the place for the first time.
Through the unknown, remembered gate
When the last of earth left to discover
Is that which was the beginning;
At the source of the longest river
The voice of the hidden waterfall
And the children in the apple-tree
Not known, because not looked for
But heard, half heard, in the stillness
between the two waves of the sea.

This earth as part of eternal exploration? Ending back where we started? Having come through the unknown but remembered gate? The hardest thing to discover is our beginning, our source? Half heard in the stillness between two eternities?

Even Shakespeare makes certain references to a more enduring spiritual reality, such as the line spoken by Hamlet: "There are more things in heaven and earth, Horatio, than are dreamt of in your philosophy" (*Hamlet*, act I, scene 5).

If the job of a poet is to put words to feelings we all partially share, to highlight and articulate the vague impressions in our souls, then those verses and others like them can kindle the glowing embers already within us.

4. "The War in Heaven" and "The Dark Prince"

The idea of a prior or mystical life in which there was a polarizing conflict persists through tales and stories old and new—battles waged for the hearts of men where the loser breaks away and becomes a dark and evil opposing force.

Wagner wrote operas with this theme, and Goethe used it as a story line. C. S. Lewis and J. R. R. Tolkien wrote stories where the greatest evil came from one who was once favored of God. Even current movie sagas like *Star Wars* and bestselling books like the Harry Potter series have themes centered on a Darth Vader or a Voldemort—a prince turned bad and now locked in conflict for the possession of our souls.

The book of Revelation, the last book in the Bible, tells in its twelfth chapter of a war in heaven where the great dragon was cast out with his followers and became the evil opponent of Christ.

Did these story lines just spring one from another or come by coincidence or happenstance? Or are they all based on a true story that each of us vaguely remembers from our dim spiritual past?

5. Scripture

Those who believe the Bible to contain sacred writing have particular and specific reasons to believe in a life before life. God Himself says to the prophet Jeremiah, "Before I formed thee in the belly I knew thee; and before thou camest forth out of the womb I sanctified thee, and I ordained thee a prophet" (Jeremiah 1:5). God is referred to in the Old Testament as "the God of the spirits of all flesh" (Numbers 27:16), and we are told that when we die the body returns to the earth and "the spirit shall return unto God who gave it" (Ecclesiastes 12:7). God implies that Job was alive when He (God) "laid the foundations of the earth . . . when the morning stars sang together, and all the sons of God shouted for joy" (Job 38:4, 7).

The New Testament book of Hebrews speaks of the "fathers of our flesh" and "the Father of spirits [God]" (Hebrews 12:9). The apostle Paul indicates that he and other followers were chosen by Christ "before the foundation of the world" (Ephesians 1:4). Jude writes of "angels which kept not their first estate" (Jude 1:6). The apostles of Christ ask him if a particular man who was blind from birth was cursed because of something he'd done before (John 9:2).

Christ himself clearly had a premortal existence. We are taught by John that Jesus "was in the beginning with God" and *later* "was made flesh" (John 1:2, 14). Christ suggested to His disciples that He would "ascend up where he was before" (John 6:62). Jesus helped create this earth (see John 1:1–3; Colossians 1:15–17), and He speaks of His own life before life when He tells His apostles that He lived before Abraham (see John 8:58) and that He came forth from the Father and would leave the world to go again to the Father (see John 16:28). In His last prayer in Gethsemane, Christ asks God to glorify Him "with the glory which I had with thee before the world was" (John 17:5). In perhaps the most direct statement of all, John says, in the New Testament, "No man hath ascended up to heaven, but he that came down from heaven" (John 3:13).

Why aren't scriptures about life before life even more prevalent and more specific and definitive? Perhaps for the same reason that scriptures about afterlife are often general and vague. Those who wrote were inspired and prophetic in glimpsing both the prelife and the afterlife but did not have complete memory or complete detail of either.

6. Early Christianity

There is substantial evidence that the concept of a premortal existence endured for some time in Christianity after the time of Paul. In the *Clementine Recognitions*, one of the earliest Christian writings after the New Testament, Clement says: "Well, if I live after, I must have lived before. Doesn't that follow?" (*Clementine Recognitions*, I, 1).

Clement also wrote of questions he had that he thought only Peter could answer. Among those questions were, "Why don't we remember the premortal existence?" "When was the world created?" and "What existed before that?" (*Clementine Recognitions*, I, 2).

The doctrine of a life before life was debated in the early Christian church in the centuries following the death of Christ's original apostles. Under pressure from the Roman emperor, Justinian, the pope consented to officially drop the belief in a premortal existence of the soul from Roman Christianity in A.D. 553 (see Philip Schaff and Henry Wace, eds., *Nicene and Post-Nicene Fathers*, Second Series, vol. XIV, Eerdmans Publishing Co., 1956, 320). Thereafter these doctrines quietly slipped from the attention and interest of most of the Christian world.

7. Reincarnation Appeal/Aversion

Immortality via reincarnation has an undeniable attraction to many and seems to match the lessons the very earth teaches us. Plants die, decompose, and regrow in similar or different forms. Déjà vu, our own and what we hear from others, seems to fit the reincarnation paradigm. And even for those who do not delve deeply into reincarnation doctrine or philosophy, there is a long-range equality or fairness suggested by passing through several lives, some rich and some poor, some privileged and some oppressed.

Yet, at the same time, something tells us we have always been who we are. To many, the idea of cycling through completely different personalities feels foreign and unlikely, even frightening and dark. Furthermore, the numbers don't work. It is likely that more people lived on earth during the twentieth century than in all previous centuries combined. There have simply not been enough earlier lives for everyone to have had a previous turn.

Nevertheless, belief in reincarnation has reached remarkably high levels in this country (Gallup says 38 percent). A contributing factor is popular contemporary books like *Old Souls* by Tom Shroder and *Many Lives, Many Masters* by Brian Weiss, which present well-documented evidence of persons who have (sometimes while under hypnosis) been able to recall obscure details from the life of another person who lived hundreds of years before—personal details that the "recaller" could never have known by "natural means." In many cases the details were confirmed and documented as accurate by after-the-fact research. Weiss, Shroder, and others conclude that this is proof that these people lived before—as other people.

They are partially right. People's recall of "unknowable"

details from others' lives *does* indicate that they lived before their birth, but it does not prove that they lived *as* those other people. Those whose lives they recall could have been friends or loved ones from the premortal existence whose earth-turns came first and whom they "watched" because of their love and interest in them. The earlier lives they recall could even be the lives of ancestors or those whose actions or fate would in some way affect their own lives when their turn on earth came. These partial or hidden spirit memories may indicate that we knew or were spiritually interested in a person who lived in an earlier time, not that we *were* that person.

I met a famous British TV personality once during a sailing trip in the Caribbean. Over dinner one night he told me that he had "converted" from Christianity to Hinduism. I asked for his reasons. "Just one," he said. "Life has always seemed extremely unfair and arbitrary to me. Some are born healthy and rich, others crippled and poor. I was having a hard time believing in a God who would allow that, until I found the Hindu explanation of reincarnation—many lives, some hard and some easy—all balancing out over time." His only regret, he said, was that he still had a feeling for the divinity of Christ.

I asked him if his hope for fairness could also be met by an eternal spirit in us that came from an earlier place, a spirit that didn't change species or identities but did go through multiple phases of existence, with one phase perhaps determining what circumstances were needed in the next. He said he supposed so, but that he had never really considered that alternative or possibility.

We do move through eternity from life to life, but we don't have to change species or personalities or bodies to do so. We stay ourselves and move through different realms.

8. Popular Modern Writers

Gary Zukav, in his bestseller, *The Seat of the Soul* (Simon and Schuster, 1989), says that "the personality can be loving, compassionate, and wise in its relations with others. But love, compassion, and wisdom do not come from the personality. They are experiences of the soul," and that "the perspective of the soul is immense," having "chosen the physical experience of life as we know it as a path of [spiritual] evolution." He talks of the soul coming "into the physical arena, into our Earth School" and says, "A conscious lifetime, therefore, is a treasure beyond value" (pp. 34–35). While Zukav believes that the soul experiences these lifetimes time after time through reincarnation, the point is that he, like so many other contemporary spiritual writers, believes in an eternal soul that predates this life and this world and that is progressing through mortal experience.

James Redfield, author of one of the most popular books of the '90s, *The Celestine Prophecy* (Warner Books, 1997), speaks of our time as one in which mankind feels a greater "urge to explore the age-old questions of life: Why are we really here? Is there a spiritual purpose underlying the struggles of human history?" In this time of spiritual awakening, Redfield claims that "each month we know more [feel more?] about the spiritual life we were living before birth and the one to which we will return after death." He says, "we came to this earth first to find the greater part of ourselves" and "we *planned* to come into this life with certain interests and momentum so that we could eventually understand and accomplish a special purpose. We came here wishing to follow a certain path. . . . Our life is not just about survival but also about spiritual evolution."

Chérie Carter-Scott, in her bestseller, *If Life Is a Game,*

These Are the Rules (Broadway Books, 1998), gets to the heart of the issue on the first page of chapter one (a chapter titled, "Rule One: You Will Receive a Body"). She says, "The moment you arrived here on this Earth, you were given a body in which to house your spiritual essence. The real 'you' is stored inside this body. . . . Though you will travel through your entire lifetime together, you and your body will always remain two separate and distinct entities. . . . If you are open to all the lessons and gifts your body has to offer you, it can impart to you valuable bits of wisdom and grace that will guide you along your path of spiritual evolution" (pp. 7–8).

Following a list of other "rules" about life and learning, Carter-Scott's last chapter is "Rule Ten: You Will Forget All of This at Birth," in which she says, "You came into this world already knowing all of the information imparted by these ten rules. You simply forgot them somewhere along your journey from the spirit world to the physical one. . . . When something resonates for you . . . you are remembering what you originally knew" (p. 124).

All three of these writers, like many current spiritual thinkers, conclude that there is a spiritual evolution under way among mankind and that we live in a new age where more spiritual questions are being asked than ever before. Answers come in a variety of forms and from a variety of sources, but they are best discerned and best believed in the context that we are eternal spirits who did not originate on this earth.

9. Inspiration, Intuition, Inclination

The answer just came out of nowhere." "I don't know how I knew, but I did." "I just felt a nudge." "I was prompted." "Something inspired me.""It was just a strong intuition." "Right then I just knew it was true."

Where do the nudgers, the promptings, the little glimpses of guidance we all occasionally feel come from? Are they old, semiforgotten memories? Are they nonverbal communication from someone else? Perhaps, but most of us associate them with spirit.

When religious people say, "I feel the spirit," what do they mean? Do they mean they feel the spirit of God—the Holy Spirit? Or do they mean that they feel their own spirits, that they are aware of something spiritual going on inside themselves? Or do they mean both—that their own spirits are feeling something that is coming from or being transmitted by the Holy Spirit?

Inspiration is indeed a transmission-reception kind of feeling. We're feeling a different part of ourselves—the most real and eternal part, a part not of our body and not of our brain. Yet what is coming to us—the inspiration or the conviction—is coming into us from outside of us, from above and beyond us.

We can feel it and receive it because of who we are and where we came from.

10. Conscience and Universal Ethics

Why, in virtually every society of every age, are there such common standards and notions about what is "good" and what is "bad"?

Answers to most other "either-or" categories have to be learned by real or vicarious experience or study. We learn much of the true-false of things in school. We learn many safe-unsafe things by trial and error. Is it possible that the right-wrong judgments that seem so obvious were also learned by experience . . . but in a life before this life?

It's not only the fact that we know right and wrong that is interesting, it's the *method* by which we know or are reminded. It is something that we call a conscience—a predictable, dependable prompting that often warns us before we make wrong choices and injects us with at least a little guilt afterwards.

What exactly is that "conscience," and where did it come from? No one programmed us. We don't have some "conscience chip" implanted surgically into our brains. Conscience isn't part of our physiology or our gray matter. Its existence and operation are evidences of the reality of our spirits. And the presence of conscience is an indication that those spirits had developed and learned much before they came to inhabit these bodies or this earth.

11. Our Tendency to Feel "Moved"

What a weird, emotional mood I must be in," I thought. Tears were welling up in my eyes and a lump was forming in my throat as I was watching gymnastics on TV. It was the 1976 Olympics, and Nadia Comaneci had just performed a routine on the uneven parallel bars that earned a score of a perfect 10. There was something so beautiful, so exquisite about it that I was moved. Her performance was not just fractionally or proportionately better than others, it was different in kind. It had crossed some invisible threshold and become almost unearthly.

Another day, walking through a park and noticing a young family—two parents, two children—walking and laughing hand in hand, I was suddenly moved to tears, touched in some deep, unexpected way.

A spectacular symphony performance, a sunset of almost impossible beauty. You can't predict when it will happen, nor can you plan it or will it to occur. But I wish it would happen more often. I love to feel moved.

What is it that actually happens when we are moved? Is it a physiological reaction of some kind, like crying when we slice onions? Is it an emotional response, like when we're startled or scared? No, it's so completely different. It feels more like spirit than body or mind.

Some things, some places, some moments—in their beauty or their perfection or their tenderness—seem to transcend what our senses can compute or comprehend. We are overcome. We use the term *moved*, which is a descriptive word because it takes us to someplace else, to another time and another place where a higher realm of beauty and perfection existed.

It's hard to explain or even to understand this phenomenon of feeling moved, but it lifts us. It is a kind of longing that reminds us of something or someone, and we sense that the wonder we feel is a wonder we once knew.

12. Our Affinity for the Earth

I sat on a deserted Hawaiian beach at first light one morning. Awakened early by the mainland time difference, I had walked along the dark sand seeking silently for the spirit's renewal of the prelife insight that comes only when there is peace and faith.

That morning the spirit came not from beyond the earth but from within it. As I sat looking east over the primordial sea, the bright dome of the sun bulged the horizon, swathing the underside billows of the clouds with yellow light and tipping the waves with gold. My heart responded to the warmth and my mind to the light, and I knew again that the earth itself is part of the answer.

We are drawn to and calmed and renewed by the beauty of the earth because it was made for us. Our spirits may even have observed its creation. Its power and majesty as well as its beauty speak to us of God and testify to us of His love and glory. The crashing music of these waves and the new morning light on the green mountain across the bay are more than the joy of the present; they are a witness of the past. Our affinity for them and for the inexhaustible variety of all the natural beauty of the physical earth is an ever-present sign of an eternal past and of a powerful and artistic Creator who is also a wise and giving Father.

Why is it so much easier to feel doubt in the noise and squalor of a city than in the silence and serenity of a seascape or a mountaintop? Because, just as a great building testifies of those who built it, so this earth testifies of Him who made it and of us who are His children. The spiritual emotion of faith is as natural here as the physical/mental emotion of doubt is there.

13. Spiritual Longing

That first-day-of-vacation Hawaiian sunrise was so glorious that I resolved to sit on that same beach every morning of my holiday at the same hour, becoming a self-taught expert on sunrises. The second morning a gray cloud bank lay low on the ocean, hiding the sun but allowing it to perform a pink, green, and gold miracle on the mackerel-patterned clouds above. I thought of our old home in England, where at this same hour this same sun was setting.

My mind was filled again with Wordsworth's words, "The soul that *rises* with us . . . hath had elsewhere its *setting.*" The sunrise of this mortal life was the sunset of our preexistent life. And when we die here, the setting of our physical lives will be the rising of our spiritual lives. And then sometime, in the most magnificent new day of all, our physical and spiritual selves will rise together in a miracle called the resurrection.

As I sit on this beach, sand crabs scurry and burrow into their holes, little needle-nosed birds dart across the wave-polished sand and pluck up food morsels, and an occasional school of tiny silver flying fish bursts briefly up and across the water's surface. All are perfectly adapted to where they live on the earth, as much a natural part of this planet as the sand or the sea. They don't need coats or air conditioning to be comfortable here—or wristwatches strapped on their appendages.

We, on the other hand, have a spiritual intuition that sometimes whispers that we are strangers here on this marvelous orbiting school of nature and experience and time—that we are spiritual, eternal beings in a physical, temporary place, adapting ourselves to the illuminating new beauty that is here yet longing deeply at times for the spiritual home we recall not with our memories but with our hearts.

14. The Logical Need for an Origin for the Spirit in Which We Believe

I've mentioned it before, but I'll mention it again in this context of a list of evidences or prompters that suggest a life before life: Most people are comfortable with a belief that there is a spirit within each of us that continues to live after the body dies. But many are uncomfortable with the question of where that spirit originated or came from. Some are even more uncomfortable with certain specific "possibilities":

1. The union of a physical sperm and egg created a spirit as well as a body.

2. A spirit somehow evolves and grows out of our minds or our brains.

3. God instantaneously generated a new spirit and put it in each body as it was born.

4. God existed alone in the universe and made people with eternal spirits to keep Himself company.

It is far more logical and "light" to believe that the spirits that postdate our bodies also predate them.

Perhaps the choice lies not in whether or not we had a pre-existence but in whether or not spirits exist at all. If they do, does it not make the most sense to assume that they have both a spiritual future and a spiritual past?

The even more fundamental question of the origin of life itself, in any form, also suggests an earlier existence. The weakest link and the hardest question in all atheistic, circumstantial, "no God, no soul" theories of existence is, "Where did *life* come from?"

15. Novels, Movies, Entertainment

Themes of ghosts, angels, and spirits from afar have always been popular. Of even more specific relevance here are themes involving the limitations of a disembodied spirit and the desires or longings of a spirit to have a temporal existence or a physical body that can feel, experience, love, and even die.

Popular movies like *Ghost*, *City of Angels*, and *Bicentennial Man* present variations on the theme of the desirability and the joy of mortal, physical, temporal experience.

In *Ghost*, the Patrick Swayze character, who has been killed, longs for his body as the vehicle with which to express his love to his wife. In *City of Angels*, Nicolas Cage plays an angel who would give up his immortality and his ability to fly "just to touch and smell her hair." And *Bicentennial Man*, adapted from an Isaac Asimov novel, is about a robot (played by Robin Williams) who, over the course of 200 years, gradually becomes a human, fulfilling his deep desire to be able to eat and sleep, to take in and appreciate beauty, to experience and express emotions, to feel love and passion, to have real choices, and ultimately to die.

Consider the frequency and the appeal of notions about the wonder and joy of accessing and possessing the physical. Might that appeal stem from a time long ago when our spirits had yet to experience mortality and all that goes with it?

16. Spiritual Differences between Siblings and the Feeling That Some Children Have "Older Souls"

I was doing some television work in a New York studio one day that involved satellite links to other locations. We would broadcast for a few minutes and then sit and wait for the link to the next location. During these breaks I had an ongoing discussion with one of the cameramen—a worldly, somewhat

crude man who essentially told me that he didn't believe in anything except himself. Yet he showed a tender affection when I
asked about his young daughter.

"What can I tell you?" he said after relating some of her
accomplishments. "She's just a special spirit. I've always had the
impression that she has an 'older soul.'"

It struck me as interesting how this self-proclaimed
nonbeliever used words like *spirit* and *impression* and *soul*. Even
more, it struck me that he sensed in his beloved little daughter
an "older soul," a part of her that knew things, that had deep
feelings, a part that seemed older than her body—even older
than himself.

I've experienced children like that, some of them my own.
I've looked into the eyes of infants and felt not only that they
had just come from another place but that their spirits were as
old as or older than mine. I've watched my own children exhibit
completely different personalities and propensities, despite the
similarities in their genetic and environmental inputs.

There is something missing in the ongoing debate about
whether it is genetics or environment that shapes a child. (I'm
reminded of the cartoon showing a red-faced father glaring at

a bad report card and his little son asking him, "What do you think it is, Dad, environment or heredity?") What's missing is the third variable, bigger and more determining than either of the others: the variable of who we were before we came, or who and what our spirits had become before they were born into mortality. This factor stands as the strongest explanation for why individual children in the same family are so deeply and profoundly different from each other.

Parents often know, if they let themselves, that there is more to their children than genetics. In the course of my research, I asked many people if they believed in a life before life. Generally, it was parents who gave the most positive and interesting responses. One mother put it most directly: "Of course I do," she said. "I have four children!"

17. Antiquity and Greek Philosophy

Philosophers throughout time have expressed the conviction that it is just as logical—if not *more* logical—to believe in a pre-life as to believe in an afterlife.

In *Phaedo*, Simmias, speaking to Socrates, says: "Yes, Socrates; I am convinced that there is precisely the same necessity for the existence of the soul before birth, and of the essence of which you are speaking: and the argument arrives at a result which happily agrees with my own notion. For there is nothing which to my mind is so evident as that beauty, goodness, and other notions of which you were just now speaking have a most real and absolute existence; and I am satisfied with the proof."

Socrates replies, "Well, but is Cebes equally satisfied? for I must convince him too."

Simmias answers: "Cebes is satisfied: although he is the most incredulous of mortals, yet I believe that he is convinced of the existence of the soul before birth. But that after death the soul will continue to exist is not yet proven" (in *The Apology, Phaedo, and Crito of Plato*, trans. Benjamin Jowett, P. F. Collier & Son Corp., 1909, p. 68).

The notion of a premortal life is an ongoing belief from very early times. Iamblichus suggests that the story of Euphorbus and the Phrygian in *Homer* offers a key to the recollection of a premortal existence. He even finds the genius of Homer to lie in his power to stir in us such "intimations of immortality," a sense of another world (see *De Vita Pythagorica* 14:63).

The substance of Greek philosophy, according to Walter Wili, was the full story of the universe, including existence in premortal, mortal, and postmortal states. Without that story, the ancient Greek perspective of life lost its meaning.

18. Fundamentals of Unique Humanness

I watched an award-winning television show in which a videographer, through his internal body-probe microphotography, was attempting to support the happenstantial cross-species theory of evolution. It showed the similarities in skeletal structure, neuron networks, and organ and reproductive function between humans and virtually every other creature—from shark to elephant. The program's conclusion: A human being is just another animal out on one branch of the evolutionary tree—more advanced than other animals in some ways, less in others.

I always wonder, when I see or read things like that, how their authors manage to dwell on such unremarkable similarities and yet to ignore completely the profound and utterly remarkable differences.

Of course there are physical similarities between the bodies of animals and humans. Why wouldn't God use similar, proven, well-designed skeletal structures in the physical vehicles He created to house His spirit children during the physical learning stage of their eternal education? Does the fact that a car has wheels prove that it evolved from an oxcart, which also has wheels? Or does it just show that the same kind of intelligence created both?

But why make it a physical question anyway? Don't all real believers stress that it is the soul or the spirit that came from God?

All animals can "think" to some degree, but only humans can think about their thoughts. Don't dismiss that as a cute or simple cliché. The ability to think about our thoughts is true human (and divine) *consciousness*. It is this consciousness of thoughts, of self, of options, of time, of plans, and of progress that makes us human. And in that context, *human* means "spiritual," and *spiritual* means "of and from God."

Our Spiritual Compass

❦ ❦ ❦ ❦ ❦

Why people know what they know (and how)

The Difference

If a person can come to a personal belief in a life before life, what difference will it make?

This is an important question because the amount of effort we put into believing something is generally directly related to the amount of benefit we feel there would be if we did believe. And believing does take effort. Although in some of its forms it comes naturally to many people, believing in a specific aspect or phase of eternity requires consciousness and concentration, pondering and prayer.

So what difference can it make to know we lived before? Chapter 5 will be devoted entirely to this question, but we may need a preview here as motivation.

If you lived before your birth, you are an eternal soul, and all the frailties and problems of this earth are temporary and likely a part of some greater plan. If you lived before, so did your friends, your children, and your spouse, and you can thus find for them a deeper respect and love. If you lived before, there is far more to you than physical genetics and a few years of trial-and-error experience; there are important and valuable parts of yourself yet to be discovered, talents, abilities, passions, and interests that started to develop very long ago; and your worth is eternal and profound, not temporary and not determined by what you did last week or last year.

The difference this knowledge can make to you is great, as are the blessings and benefits of believing, and the questions of *how* to believe are worth asking.

A "Ring of Truth"

The story is told of a man whose family was killed in Eastern Europe at the beginning of World War II. The man, who was only a small child at the time, had survived and been taken into France by escaping refugees. He ended up in an orphanage and was eventually adopted and raised by American parents in California. The orphanage had no records other than a note that he had been rescued as a toddler from somewhere in Eastern Europe.

Many years later, the man developed a powerful interest in his roots and a desire to discover where he had come from. Finally, when he had some financial resources, he took a leave of absence from his work and went to Europe, determined to do whatever he had to to find his childhood home. His only memory, and it was just a shred, was of a church tower that must have been near his house—a church with a bell that he woke to as he would lie in his crib.

So he traveled across Poland, through Hungary and Bulgaria, looking and listening, trying to recall or to recognize something, somewhere. As weeks turned to months, he visited hundreds of cities, villages, and towns and listened to literally thousands of church bells, each unique and beautiful, but none of which awakened anything familiar in him.

Finally, discouraged and convinced that he simply didn't have enough evidence to work with, he made plans to return home. He booked a flight for the following week and decided to spend his last few days visiting some tiny villages in a very rural and remote sector.

Early the next morning, only four days before he was to leave, he pulled his rental car into a little town, parked, got out, and was walking toward a bakery when he heard his bell. He knew the instant he heard it that this was his childhood home.

The years fell away, and he heard the bell just as he had from his crib. It was unmistakable. He was home.

Spiritual truth, when we hear it, can ring as clearly and recognizably as the bell in that story. Because we are spiritual beings, we have spiritual memories, memories that are dim but not gone, veiled but not blocked. Thus spiritual truths resonate; they *feel* right. They ring true. They have about them a spiritual logic and light.

In contrast, lies and spiritual deceptions carry a dissonant, unfamiliar ring and seem to project a kind of darkness.

We can learn to trust spiritual ideas and messages and impressions that fill our souls with light and love, with hope and joy . . . and to turn away from spiritual notions that cloud our thoughts or carry a sense of confusion or delusion.

You can *develop* your ability to recognize and respond to spiritual light and to more clearly "hear" the ring of spiritual truth. It is a little like tuning in to a faint radio signal. If you ignore or disregard or fail to value it because it is faint, it will fade away. But if you recognize and acknowledge that you "heard" (felt) something and work at getting it to come through more clearly (asking for help, tuning, turning yourself in different directions, listening harder), you begin to tune in and the message becomes more clear.

Ways of Knowing

Seeing is believing," the old saying goes, and indeed it is our five senses that give us most of our knowledge about the things around us. We see and hear our world—we taste it and touch it and smell it. We begin to equate reality with the things our physical senses can perceive, and we sometimes tend to categorize everything else as illusion.

In other moments, though—actually in our finest moments—we know that there are other ways of knowing. It is not our five senses that tell us that we love someone or that we feel truly loved. And it is not our senses, though they may supply some of the input, that tell us that we have a soul and that there is a higher power who gave us our senses to help us perceive and experience His other gifts. This kind of knowing is more pure and more sure than anything that can come through our senses—and it is less subject to confusion or to delusion.

Although we often think of our senses as the most reliable

realizers of reality, they are actually the least trustworthy. How many times have you heard (or said), "I thought I saw something." Our eyes and our ears are easily fooled. Magicians make a living on sensory illusion. The things we know most truly come from a place deeper inside us and from a source higher above us.

My emotional knowledge that I love my wife and children is deeper and surer than any physical knowledge. Closely linked and another step beyond emotional knowledge is the spiritual knowledge of God and of who we really are and who we always have been.

Emotional knowledge is stronger than physical knowledge, but it is also harder to come by. It's effortless to look at or listen to something and know that it's there. To truly love someone or to fully accept another's love for us takes more effort and more time.

Spiritual knowledge, the third and highest form of knowing, is still deeper and still harder. It is two levels harder than seeing or hearing and one level beyond loving. The reason it is harder is that it involves and is built on faith—on accepting and trusting in things that are above and beyond the common, physical, everyday experience of this world.

But here is the irony: Although exercising faith is hard, claiming its absence may well be harder. To believe in what we cannot see or touch is sometimes difficult, but to not believe is at times—at very good times—virtually impossible. In those moments of exquisite beauty or profound love or quiet inspiration, we cannot give ourselves credit, nor can we deny credit to some higher, brighter, fuller source. This is why most people believe in God—because, in balance, it is easier and more natural and ultimately more logical to believe than not to believe.

There is a wonderful binary quality about spiritual knowledge. Either there is a God or there isn't. Either our souls continue after death or they don't. Either our spirits lived before their birth or they didn't. This yes-or-no, on-or-off, true-or-false reality can nourish our faith. When we ponder something and wish to know if it is true, we can "try" both sides spiritually. We can assume and believe a thing and see if that belief generates light or darkness in our minds. A belief that sparks enlightenment and further insight can be invited to linger and grow, while a notion that prompts darkness, fear, confusion, or repulsion can be rejected and dismissed.

Our Spiritual Compass

Useful as this spiritual toggle switch is—the one that responds with light or dark to spiritual questions—we have another built-in "spiritual instrument" that may help us even more. It is a kind of spiritual compass that will, if we let it, point us in the direction of our individual spiritual destiny.

God's commitment to our agency does not lessen His interest in us or His desire that we find truth and discover and develop the best that is within us. Providing us with a road map would supersede our need for the very faith and independence that draw us close to Him. But a compass, something that points in the right direction in response to our request, preserves our initiative and allows the thrill of discovery.

Our spiritual compass works in a clear and simple way, but only according to our needs and our requests. It works as a conscience when we face moral decisions. It works like a magnetic pole in prayer about big life-choices. And it turns us toward beacons of light as we ponder and pray about spiritual purpose and the reasons for life.

Yet, like some kind of battery-powered direction finder, our spiritual compass can spin at random until it is plugged into the current of faith. We must strive to believe in it and in the source of its power. The moment we take it for granted, it will fail us.

You can recognize and apply your spiritual compass as you think about a life before life. Hold the concept up in your heart and see if it reflects spiritual light. Pray and ask about your eternity and your soul, and let your compass point you toward the peace and purpose of believing.

I hate to hear people say, "Spirituality is a crutch. Believing is for people who are too weak to accept reality." Spirit *is* reality, as is God—the strongest, surest reality of all. And believing takes strength and faith and mental and spiritual effort. The weak, easy thing is not to know if you believe, to default the whole question because it is too hard to seek and find answers. The crutch is agnosticism, the cop-out of marking the "I don't know" or "None of the above" box.

Be open to spiritual truth. Ask and activate your spiritual

compass. Then trust it. Allow yourself to believe things that feel right, that ring true, that add light.

Asking

Questions are powerful things. Real questions that we ask because we really want answers are anything but passive. They focus the attention of the asker. They demand the attention of the "askee." They motivate action and searching.

When we ask any of the big three questions mentioned earlier (Where did I come from? Why am I here? Where am I going?), *who* are we asking, either directly or by implication? We are asking God! Whether we realize it or not, we are asking God or whatever our concept of Divinity is. That we even ask the questions or that they even come to our minds is a small but pure evidence that we believe in Him who is the only One who could give us an answer.

Asking often enough and hard enough yields answers. This is not casual or hypothetical asking, not asking an encyclopedia or the Internet. It is asking God and asking the deepest part of ourselves.

The most frequent, oft-repeated, and reiterated admonition

in all of scripture is to *ask*. "Ask and ye shall receive," we are promised again and again. A God who loves us yet who is committed to our *agency* and freedom of choice (who in fact made this earth to give us that agency, freedom, and independence) would not interfere or intervene in ways that would remove that freedom or undermine our initiative. But when we *ask*, we are exercising that initiative, and a loving God can *answer* and *bless* without interfering or compromising our agency.

The Process of Believing

Reading about and thinking for the first time about life before life is a little like walking on deep, crusted snow. In some places the footing is strong and sure, other spots are slippery, and in some places the crust is thin and we break through and fall. But with a little time, and with the snowshoes of faith and prayer, the journey to belief and reassurance can be made. It is a worthy destination because we arrive with a deeper self-worth and a wider love than we have ever known.

The process of believing, of spiritual knowing, is the same for you and me. As I have searched and read and thought and prayed, I have believed the things that have *fit with what I feel*.

That fit, of information with inclination, of feeling with faith, is the key to spiritual knowing—a knowing that is more sure than any sight or any sound.

Natural Faith

There is within you much that is unique, much about how you think and how you feel that cannot be explained merely by heredity or environment. You are who you are because you have *become* that way, little by little, over eternity. Your gifts and talents as well as your weaknesses and faults have developed over an unimaginable span.

Within your spirit is a conscience, an innate sense of right and wrong and of spiritual light and dark, a propensity to believe and to acknowledge the spiritual. This conscience and these spiritual propensities can be blunted and dulled by inattention or denial, or they can be sharpened and fine-tuned, even magnified, by belief and by faith.

Faith, in that context, is a fascinating concept. It is not a belief in something completely beyond us. It is a belief in something *within* us. As we learn and believe spiritual truth, it feels rather more like remembering than like discovering.

Thus believing and faith are partially a product of *wanting* or *desiring*. We each have spiritual capacity because our essence *is* spirit. But here, clothed in our physicality, our spirit selves can be denied and diminished if we do not allow ourselves to believe, if we do not want to believe.

Allowing Yourself to Believe

Believe in God, believe in your own spirit, believe there is more to you than physical genetics, believe that you came from a spiritual premortal existence. Believing is the conscious act of will that is the beginning of faith. Spiritual believing is a natural thing for a spiritual being.

Believe that we have within us some divine spark, some God-sent spirit that separates us from animals and from the rest of the physical world. Animals become all they can be by following their instincts and obeying their appetites. Humans become all they can be by disciplining and mastering and controlling their appetites and by believing in something beyond.

There is no weakness in wanting to believe. In fact, that desire is the source of our greatest strength. The inclination of your spirit self to believe is as natural as the inclination of your physical self to eat.

Allow yourself to believe—not just in the possibility of some vaguely defined superior being or of an occasional spiritual inclination within yourself. Believe in the real God who is your Heavenly Father and in an earth with a purpose and in your own eternal spirit, which came from and can return to God.

Intermission: Kilimanjaro and Kolob

☙ ☙ ☙ ☙ ☙

Deciding to write about life before life

In a play or a concert, the intermission gives you a chance to stretch, perhaps to reflect a little on the first act and anticipate the second.

I'd like this intermission to do the same for you. Thinking generally about the possibility of a life before life and of the impact that such a belief could have on you is one thing. Going deeper into what that premortal existence consisted of and actually applying it to your life is something else again.

If I expect you to go deeper with me, it seems I ought to tell you a bit more of my personal experience—of how and why I came to write this book.

In other words, if you know a little more about "where I'm coming from," it may feel more natural to tell you more about where I believe I (and you) came from.

The Prompting

For years I had struggled with it. A prompting that I resisted but that wouldn't go away. "Write what you know about life before life. Share the light you've been given."

The impressions came repeatedly and at random, unexpected times: watching a young family in a restaurant; driving across a desert into an orange and purple sunset; once at night in a dream so potent it woke me and kept me up, thinking, for the rest of the night. *"Give what you've received. People need to know what you know about the life before."* Once in a bookstore I picked up a copy of the book *Life After Life*, and as I turned it over in my hands it seemed for just an instant that I saw on the back of the book another title, *Life Before Life*.

I resisted the promptings because I wasn't sure if anyone was interested, and most of all because I didn't think I could find words to express what I feel and know. After all, I write books about goal setting, life balance, parenting—practical things, things people know they need, things you can give people methods for, things you can explain with examples and stories. I wasn't ready . . . wasn't even capable of writing about the soul.

But the promptings didn't go away, and gradually they turned into a desire. When I would sit down to work on other books, my mind would wander and I would find my pen scrawling thoughts about the nature of premortal life and the purpose of this mortal life.

I began to realize that these thoughts, regardless of how many people were interested, were vastly more important than the other things I was writing. Gradually the conviction came that I had to try to write them, whether anyone would ever read them or not.

A new millennium was beginning. The promptings became more specific: *"Write it now."* There is no better time for looking forward and backward than at a millennial change. The awe of a new thousand years releases us a little from the mundane present—allows us glimpses into a higher realm of reflection and perspective.

It occurred to me that to write about something so removed from the here-and-now I would have to remove myself from the familiar comfort zone of the day-to-day and go some-place where I could think with perspective and clarity about what I had come to know about the eternities. Where, though? Where and how would I find the words?

During the time that I was having these thoughts and questions, our family was planning a trip to Eastern Africa to participate in some humanitarian work in a group of primitive villages in Kenya. I suppose that a part of my motivation for going was the hope that such a dramatic change of scenery and of perspective might somehow help me get started on the writing I now felt I had to do. There was also an option, while we were in the vicinity, to climb Mt. Kilimanjaro, the massive and picturesque highest peak on the African continent. As we read about how difficult the climb was, and how much time and expense it required, we realized that there were a lot of reasons not to go. But there was something about the challenge that I couldn't resist, something that I felt might be related to my questions about how and what to write.

So I would go. I would follow the promptings and see if, on that place half a world away, I could find the words to share what I had to share, the reality and empowerment of an earlier place and time from which all of us came.

The Mountain

Mt. Kilimanjaro sits right on the equator near the border between Kenya and Tanzania. At 19,400 feet, it is the highest peak in Africa, and because it rises so singularly from the relatively low and flat African plain, it has been called the most impressive mountain in the world. It certainly impressed me.

You see it first from nearly fifty miles away, a snowy mound pushing impossibly high above the green jungle horizon. As we bumped along the rutted Kenyan roads, I couldn't take my eyes off the mountain looming larger and larger. The previous two weeks in the small Kenyan villages and the vast Massai Mara Plain had humbled me and placed me in a grateful, thoughtful mood and mind frame.

That night, as we stayed in some small climbers' cabins at the base of the mountain, a brilliant moon rose directly above the white, glacier-covered dome of Kilimanjaro, and I said a simple prayer—a prayer about how to present spiritual reality in a way that readers could recognize as truth. No answer came that night, but I knew I was in the right place and asking the right question.

It takes five long days to climb Kili and a day and a half to come down. Each of the five climbing days is completely different from the others in its challenge and in its climate and terrain. The first day you climb through a rain forest, a wet jungle filled with vines and birds and monkeys—Tarzan's

Africa. The greater altitude of the second day brings you to a semiarid desert—scrubby little trees and dry, sparse grass. The third day you feel the mass of the mountain suspended above you, and the terrain is tundra—no trees at all, just delicate, low-lying bushes. The fourth day is like walking on the moon—nothing but gray dust and boulders. And the fifth day you are climbing on a glacier, sliding and slogging at nearly 20,000 feet toward the rocky outcropping that is the top. The sixth day, coming down, is perhaps the hardest of all.

Day One

I hoped for answers or insights on the first day, but it was hard to focus on anything other than the overwhelming beauty of the jungle—the vibrant abundance of an earth I believe was created for us.

But how could I approach and discuss that creation? Questions of creation tend to be polarizing and divisive. How could I skirt that debate and prompt readers to think about the origin of their *spirits* rather than their bodies? If I was to write about premortal life, where should I start? What was the most logical, easy-to-believe part of what I knew? What fit best with what most people already believed?

I stopped, alone, for a few moments in a clearing, watching a family of ringtail monkeys high above in the jungle canopy. My questions were in the air, suspended in my mind as before, but now there was an answer, or the first part of an answer:

"Tell them that the spirit that continues to live after physical death also lived before physical birth."

I realized that the very jungle I was standing in illustrated that fact—the fact of the regeneration and ongoing continuity of life. I knew that fact was the place to start, that I must begin with a logical extension of what most people already believed. Those who believe there is a spirit in us—a spirit that continues after death—can be prompted to think about where that spirit came from. Few would conclude that the physical merger of a sperm and egg would create a spirit. The first step in believing in life before life is realizing that our spirits came from somewhere.

Forget for a moment the questions of how and when this magnificent earth was made. Focus on why it was made. Ponder the possibility that it was made for our spirits, spirits that preexisted and that came into our bodies much as they will one day go out of our bodies.

I thought about that for the rest of the day as we climbed up out of the rain and mist of the dense jungle, and by the time we camped I knew what I wanted to put in the first chapter of this book.

Day Two

The second day was as dry as the first day had been wet. It was an easy walk on firm, hard, arid ground, the trail winding up past smaller and smaller altitude-dwarfed trees. I'd never seen a desert quite like this, yet it was pleasant and somehow familiar.

I loved the answer parts that had come yesterday, but they were just a preface. The real "how"—how to say it, in what order to tell it—was still murky. How do you figuratively walk up to someone and say, "I know something about you that you don't know"? Where is the credibility, the common ground that will make people want even to read it, let alone believe it?

I was trekking along right behind Charles, a big, jovial Tanzanian who was our head guide and who had climbed the mountain a dozen times. As we walked, we talked, and something he said in his broken English triggered part two of my answer. "I remember every time I climb," he said. "Even first time it seem like I remember it. I think I made for this mountain."

There is a lot that people know, I thought, a self-knowledge they just have, aptitudes and interests that seem to come from nowhere, a spiritual sense inside them, so that learning sometimes feels more like remembering. It's like this stark, lovely desert terrain—new yet somehow friendly and familiar.

Suddenly I had the second answer in my sequence:

"Tell them what they already know but don't quite know that they know."

There is so much scripture about life before life, so much poetry and myth about a premortal realm. And we ourselves, when the mood and the emotion are right, know we are something beyond our bodies and our brains—something older and more enduring.

It is possible to know something and not know that you know it. What I would need to do in the second part of the book would be to prompt people to look inside themselves and see what's already there, to reassure them that the concept of a premortal life is a very old one, traceable to nearly every culture and time.

I walked in silence behind Charles for a while, pondering this black brother of mine, a man with whom I had almost nothing in common . . . or maybe a man with whom, like every man, I had everything in common. And I know what I would put in chapter two.

Day Three

Tundra is the term they use in Alaska to describe vegetation so fragile that you hate to step on it. At day-three altitude no trees can grow—just scrubby, delicate little bushes here and there. Looking around, you can hardly imagine how it grows at all, in such thin soil and such thin air.

By now we were at the very upper edge of the vegetation line. Breathing was harder and slower. Everything, it seemed, was slowing down, except for my thoughts, which seemed to race.

The answers of the last two days had evolved into another series of questions that I pondered to the rhythm of my trudging steps: "How can I persuade people that there is more to them than physical genetics? What kind of reasoning or logic can lift people above their physical, day-to-day concerns enough that they will accept and believe in who they really are?"

I realized on day three how much I wanted people to believe the way I did. The perspective of a preearth existence is a thing of tremendous beauty to me, a thing that has made a profound difference in how I live and how I think. I began to feel a sort of desperate need to make it easily acceptable, a pressure to make it all compelling and believable.

I was more aware of the brilliant blue sky that third day. It stretched on endlessly, out over the vast African plain. And as I stared into its blue depth, the next part of the answer configured itself in my mind:

"Tell . . . just tell. Do not try to convince, compel, contend, or convert. Simple truth will do all that by itself."

I realized that once again my answer had come partially from where I was. This beautiful, sparse tundra was so much simpler than the jungle below. It was vivid and basic; it needed no embellishment. And so were the truths about life before life.

Maybe it was the altitude, maybe the thinner air actually weighs less, but this third answer seemed to lift a weight from my shoulders. My task was not to make a case or convince a jury, it was simply to tell what I believed of life before life, to tell it straightforwardly and clearly and to let its truth speak for itself to any who would truly listen.

Day Four

Early on day four, at breakfast, Charles laid out the plan for our final ascent. By the end of today, he said, we would be at a rock field below the base of the glacier. We would sleep for about three hours, get up just after midnight, and climb for seven or eight hours up the steep white ice to the top of the world. He detailed the route and told us about the parts we would do on our own and the parts where we would need his help and that of the other guides. There was a buzz of excitement as we prepared to ascend.

As I listened to Charles, my mind was still on this book, and I realized that the heart of what I had to say was about a plan I believe God has for us that involved our descent into mortality. There were parts of that plan that we had to implement and carry out on our own, and that was the reason for a physical life without memory of what went before. There were other parts of the plan that could not be accomplished without His self-sacrificing help. There was exhilaration and excitement as we prepared to descend.

Later that morning, as we trudged along, I asked Charles a question. We were above all vegetation now, and it looked and felt like we were walking on the moon, stepping over gray boulders and kicking up fine, gray dust.

"Why do we start the final ascent tomorrow at 1:00 A.M.? Why do we trudge most of the way up the glacier in pitch-black darkness?"

Charles smiled, as if it were a question he was used to. "See last day sunset better from up on glacier," he said.

I wasn't buying it. The final ascent would take about eight hours. "Why don't we get a good sleep tonight, get up and leave early—say at 5:00 A.M.—and get up there by early afternoon?" I asked. "We could watch the sunrise on the way up."

Charles came up with another answer: "Glacier too soft in afternoon, harder to walk on." I raised an eyebrow, so he tried a third answer, the lamest of all: "You don't get too tired in the dark."

We kept trudging up through the moonscape, and Charles

could evidently sense that I didn't like his answers. Suddenly he stopped and turned to face me. "Okay, I tell you true why we go at night," he said. "If you see where we going, you don't go."

That gave me something to think about for the rest of day four. And the thoughts tied magically into the bigger answers I had come here to find. We came into this earth from a better place, or at least an easier place. If from that place we could have seen our lives in preview, all the pain and all the trial, we may not have come. And if we could remember the place from whence we came, we might consider killing ourselves just to get back home, and we would not develop the faith and the independence we were sent here to gain.

So there is a reason we know as little as we do of life before life. But knowing that we *were* there, and knowing why we were sent here, can make every part of this life more meaningful.

Tomorrow we would start in the middle of the night and we would make most of the ascent in darkness, but at least we would know where we started and why we were climbing. And with that came the fourth part of my answer:

"Tell them what they don't know . . . and how to believe."

This was the heart of what I'd come to the mountain to

find. I knew now that in the right sequence, after reminding readers of what they already knew, I could tell them without fear about what else I've come to know about our life before life, about the relationships we had in that premortal life, and about God's plan for our eternal progress. Most importantly, I could tell them how to believe it. I knew how because I knew, and that would be the fourth chapter of the book.

That evening as the sun set, I looked down—impossibly far down on the tops of the clouds below. Most of my answer had come; most of the mountain was climbed. We would sleep three or four hours and then make the final ascent.

Day Five

The night ascent was awesome—and incredibly difficult. I began to believe Charles. I would not be doing this if I could see it. With a new moon, only the brilliant stars in the black, spacelike sky illuminated the vast, vertical mass of the mountain above us. For the first part of the night we walked through gravelly scree and slid back a half step for every forward step we took. Nearing 19,000 feet, the air was so thin that I was taking a deep, complete, inhale-exhale breath for every single step I took. It was incredibly slow and cold, but exquisitely beautiful. By about 3:00 A.M. we were on the glacier itself, picking our steps carefully as we moved up the frozen white mass.

Resting became an interesting phenomenon. If you don't stop to rest (and to drink) every hundred steps or so, you increase your chances of altitude sickness. But if you rest too long, the desire to quit and turn back becomes incredibly strong.

About halfway up the glacier, light began to gather, and then I witnessed the most glorious sunrise of my life. It turned the tops of the clouds below into burnished gold and lit the vast African plain beyond. With the sun came new energy for the final push and new assurance within that I could write the book, that people would read it, and that it could make a difference. It was more a reassurance than an answer to a question:

"Belief in life after life gives us hope.

Belief in life before life gives us worth."

I sensed during that final ascent that self-worth, self-respect, self-identity, and self-value are the key benefits of knowing our spiritual past. As important as hope and encouragement are, they don't work very well unless they are connected to worth. Even in the physical, temporal sense, it's fine to say, "You can do it . . . you can get there . . . you can endure," but unless there is a certain base level of confidence and self-worth, we don't really believe we can. Spiritually it is the same. Hope in a heaven, in a life beyond, in the inherent goodness and immortality of our souls can be hollow and distant unless we believe that we came from somewhere, that we have deep spiritual potential, and that this mortal life has real meaning and purpose.

We inched our way along a high ridge and up a black rock outcropping to the pinnacle. The top of the world. A feeling like no other, standing there, turning slowly, 360 degrees, seeing forever in every direction. I was asking the final question, "What is the ultimate purpose of this book? Why do I have to write it? Why do people need to read it? How do I explain the purpose of knowing?"

As I looked down onto the mountain beneath me— beyond the bottom of the glacier, beyond the rock field, down into the mist below—the clouds billowed and shifted, and for just a minute I caught a glimpse of the jungle nearly 20,000 feet down. There was the place we'd started from five days before, the place we would soon return to. It was the physical equivalent of the spiritual glimpses I had had of the life before, brief but sure, incomplete but comforting and beautiful. The clouds shifted again and the glimpse was gone. Having seen it, though, even dimly and briefly, made a difference. It was clearer to me where I was now, and why I had come. My brief glimpse down had brought the fifth part of my answer up:

"Tell them how knowing about living before can change everything about living now."

Perception was the key. Just as I could see more because I had been taken here to this high view, readers would see more of life and of purpose if the fifth part of the book could take them back to where they came from, where a longer view of themselves and of God's purpose could give them both hope and worth.

On the magnificence of that mountain and in the clarity of that moment, I perceived the difference such an idea could make . . . to a parent who now sees his or her children as God's children and as spiritual equals . . . to a wife who now sees her husband as someone she may have known before this life . . . to a man who now sees his worries and challenges as part of what he was sent here to learn, and views others' problems similarly, without judgment.

It was *faith* and *insight* that I wanted to share, but I saw that the real and practical gift may be *worth* and *perspective*.

Day Six

Coming down was harder than going up—harder on the knees, harder to balance, seemingly longer, and somehow steeper. Accumulated fatigue and the need to cover so much more ground made the last day the most difficult. We didn't know it at the time, but the constant flexing and slipping and pounding cracked the cartilage in Linda's knee, necessitating orthopedic surgery after we got back.

Still, despite the challenge, there was a newfound joy on day six. We were going down. We had accomplished the summit, and each of us knew that we would never be quite the same. What we had done could make a difference in our lives, if we would let it. I realized as I slid and stumbled and worked my way down that I could use this experience to change and improve how I faced other challenges.

With that thought came my sixth answer:

"Tell them how premortal insight can be applied to how we perceive and how we live."

If I stayed conscious of what I had learned on this mountain, I could apply its lessons in ways that could clear my paradigm and enhance my perspective. The final chapter of the book had to be a "how-to" section—how to use the insight to change our lives.

Four Months Later

Now an admission and an apology. Even after the answers of Kilimanjaro, I resisted. I came home to the everyday, and what I knew I had to do seemed too far away and too distant from my writing confidence. I gravitated back to other manuscripts and writing projects. I still wanted most to write about life before life, but the confidence and clarity of Kilimanjaro was slipping away.

Then in late October I went to play basketball and run track events in the world Senior Olympics, held in the red rock canyon country where Utah, Arizona, and Nevada meet. It's the perfect time of year there with the golden cottonwood and yellow aspen trees accenting the pine-covered hills beneath the massive red cliffs.

My basketball team made it to the finals against the senior team from Russia, big, raw-boned players, some of whom as younger men had played on the USSR's Olympic gold-medal team. Going up for a rebound in the second half, I caught an elbow across the bridge of my nose and blacked out briefly, barely managing to keep my feet. I tried to shake off the blow and reentered the game. Afterward, though, I felt dizzy and began to experience some clear, watery drainage from my nose that worried me. I went to see a neurologist, who worried me even more by telling me about the cribriform plate behind the nose that, if cracked, can leak cerebral/spinal fluid and allow bacteria to enter the brain from the nasal passages, sometimes causing meningitis. But he examined me neurologically and found nothing abnormal. He was particularly pleased to find that my sense of smell was in order. Smell, he told me, was often affected by a cribriform crack. He said that he doubted serious trauma but would set up an MRI and a CAT scan the following day if I wanted to be sure.

I drove back that night to where I was staying, beneath the

2,000-foot red cliffs of Kolob Canyon, part of Zion's National Park. But I didn't enjoy the beauty very much. I was preoccupied with the possibility of a brain drain.

During the night my thoughts returned to the book I had been prompted to write—perhaps it was my way of getting my mind off my mind. I prayed with the sincerity we seem to summon when there is a potentially serious worry.

The next day I felt a clear assurance that I would be fine and an impression that instead of going to the radiology section of the hospital, I should get out by myself into the majestic canyons. I saddled up an Appaloosa horse named Banner and took a ride beneath the five fingers of Kolob.

They look like the five splayed-out fingers of a massive hand, five towering, pointed cliffs of warm red rock jutting out overhead into the cool, deep, autumn-blue sky, connected to a "wrist" of a sheer red cliff. As I rode, my mind was taken back—*taken* (I didn't take it) to the six impressions of Kilimanjaro. Each of the huge red fingers and the massive connected cliff suddenly represented one of the six parts of what I had felt to say.

I looked up at the first finger and felt the words, "*Tell them that the spirit that continues to live after physical death also lived before physical birth."*

I shifted my gaze to the second massive rock finger and felt, *"Reassure them first about the parts they already know but don't quite know that they know."* Then the third: *"Tell . . . just tell. Don't try to convince or contend or convert. The truth will do all that by itself."*

The fourth red finger spoke to me: *"Tell them what they don't know—and how to believe."* And the fifth, *"Tell them how knowing about living before can change everything about living now."*

My eyes progressed to the towering, adjoining wrist-cliff of Kolob, and I felt the final message strongest of all: *"Tell them how premortal insight can be applied to how we see and how we live!"*

I rode back to where I was staying, unsaddled Banner, and sat on the porch in a rocking chair, looking up at the sun's last rays lighting Kolob, then at the moon rising as I began to write the preface.

Our Spiritual
Past

❧ ❧ ❧ ❧ ❧

What most people don't yet know (but can)

The Premortal Realm

Ａs I expand on what I have come to believe about our spiritual prelife, I will state my beliefs simply, as they have come to me, and as fact. After my experiences on Kilimanjaro and at Kolob, directness is the only approach I can take. As you read, please let your own spirit ponder at each point the possibility of its being true.

ʊ ʊ ʊ

You lived, as did I, as did everyone, long before we were born on this earth. In fact, we lived before there was an earth. We are not products of this earth, nor did we evolve from it, nor were we made to live on it. Rather, it was made for us to live on. This earth is God's handiwork, but we are God's offspring.

Our earlier home was a spiritual place of vast scope and scale, possessing a kind of macro beauty indescribable in words, unthinkable now in our micro physical minds. There is nothing here to compare it with, though I have at times felt a haunting familiarity when I have looked at the image of our bright green and blue jewel-like earth in the black of space in a picture taken from the moon, or at the Hubble telescope photos of vast swirling galaxies or brilliant exploding novas.

More important than how things looked from there is how we felt. We were something akin to children or to students. We were a different kind of being in a different level of reality. We were not independent or self-determining in the ways we think of those words now. Our options were more limited; we did not completely control our destiny. But we were separate and unique individuals with opinions and preferences of our own.

We were spirits, and our spirits had form and identity. We, and the environment in which we lived, were composed of spiritual matter—a brighter, different, more refined type of substance and energy than what we now know. We were surrounded by the physical matter of the universe as it then existed, but we could not handle or control or interact with it. This was somewhat the reverse of here and now where we, as physical matter, can sense spiritual elements around us but can't interact or relate directly to them.

There, as spirits, our thoughts were the main reality. We were a little like science pupils in the theory-and-idea-dominated classroom, yet to attend or experience the laboratory. We had yet to handle the elements or try the experiments.

As we ponder and pray from here, from our present physical reality, we can get only to feelings and glimpses—the positive reality of some of the perceptions and some of the limits of premortal life, but few of the details of it. And with these glimpses comes a sense of warning: Do not seek more than that. There is a reason for spiritual forgetfulness while in mortality. Our purpose, God's purpose in sending us here, has to do with our development of faith and independence. We must find ourselves here rather than remembering ourselves there. But knowing we *were* there, and knowing some of the purpose and plan in coming here, can help us find our truest selves.

In that spiritual, prephysical existence, you lived, as did I, and grew and progressed over a span too vast for us to grasp from here. You were an individual. You have always been separate, unique, and distinct from other spirits, developing your own character and characteristics, your own personality and propensities through your own circumstances and choices.

You knew and associated with other spirits and with God. Indeed, you were part of God's family. You referred to Him as Father because He *is* the Father of your spirit. Despite the number of spirits involved, there was an intimacy in your relationship. Nothing was limited by time because time did not exist. You had relationships with other spirits, some of whom were especially close and dear, who loved you as you loved them.

The Plan

At a pivotal point in this life before life, God, our spiritual Father, presented to us a plan for the next phase of our eternal progression—a masterful, comprehensive plan that both thrilled and terrified us.

The plan called for a new kind of existence in a new and very different kind of place. We would leave our Father and our spiritual home and take on physical bodies to populate a physical world. The world would be a remarkable place, filled with exquisite beauty and joy but also ugliness and pain. We would have a virtually unlimited number and combination of options from which to choose. We would descend into a realm of time and of maturation, deterioration, and renewal, none of which we had yet experienced. Perhaps most remarkable of all, we would become parents, participating with God in the creation of physical bodies for others of our spirit siblings who would come to earth as our children. We would then have stewardship over the growth and progress of those other spirits, just as our parents had for us. Prior to this, parenthood had been God's exclusive prerogative.

You and I felt the overwhelming anticipation and excitement of an entire new sphere of experience. But we also felt the keen apprehension of unprecedented risk. We stretched to grasp the reality of taking on a makeup and mind so different and far away that our spirit home—and our own spirit selves—would scarcely be remembered, only in vague, brief glimpses if at all. In fact, we were told that a veil of spiritual forgetfulness was a necessary and integral part of this physical laboratory—that the mortal experience (or experiment) would not serve its growth and independence-creating purpose if we could remember the details of our origin and rely on past spiritual experience. Eternal apron strings would have to be cut if we were to find and learn to rely on our deeper selves. We worried whether we would remember those we knew, whether we would find each other during our mortal lifespans, whether our physical lives would overlap in the new elements of time and geography.

Despite the trepidation we all felt, there was joy in contemplating the prospect of mortality. We would live among and experience physical matter. We would go out of the classroom's theory and into the laboratory's reality. We would experience more and feel more than ever before! We would face risk and chance and daily choice. We would learn to live and to love in ways we had never known. We would live within a realm of time, and we would die.

The best earthly analogy for what we must have felt (though it falls far short) is that of a grown child going off to college or university. He has lived with his family for many years, loving and learning in the protected environment of the home and the guiding presence of parents. But the time comes when living there longer would be counterproductive to growth. So the child, feeling more trepidation than he shows, leaves for school—to a riskier, freer environment where he is much more on his own. Choices are his, and parents hope from afar that what he has become, what he has taken with him from them, will help him choose wisely. He can call home—the phone is there—and parents encourage him to do so, wanting him still to need them even as he learns to rely ever more on himself. As time passes, the child becomes more like his parents, experiencing more and more of the same things they have experienced, so that when he sees them again, their relationship has changed. He knows them better, having done some of what they have done. Ironically, sometimes it is only by leaving someone that we can ultimately become closer to them. When a student goes away to school, he hopes to return as more than he was when he left.

With similar hopes, you and I and everyone else in his or her turn got ready to go away to this incredible orbiting school—this world of contrasts and conflicts, of opposites and options.

The hope we felt was tempered, even undercut, by a sense of ominous danger and risk. We felt strongly the worry and the threat of not returning. We knew that God's realm was one of perfection, and we saw and understood how the imperfection inherent in the physicality and freedom of this place could disqualify us to come back, could taint us in ways that would make us inconsistent, incompatible, or incapable of a return. Still, the predominant feelings were excitement and joy.

Purpose

Part of the excitement we felt as we anticipated mortality came from the clarity with which we understood *why* we were going to earth.

Excitement is always heightened when purpose or mission is crystal clear and specific. Astronauts, for example, talk of how keen their anticipation is as they make preparations for a space mission and know the precise reasons for going and the exact things they are expected to accomplish. Elements of danger and difficulty also enhance the "high" as they get ready to blast out of this world and up into space.

Magnified a million times, that is the sort of keen, joyful anticipation our spirits felt as we came to understand the awesome purposes of blasting out of eternity and down into this world. We would form new kinds of relationships, based on mutual *needs*, and feel new kinds of love involving interdependency, service, and physical attraction—love we would be able to express with completely new kinds of personal intimacy.

The contrast of these temporal possibilities with our spiritual existence was so sharp that it took the equivalent of our spiritual breath away. Relationships on a whole new scale. Experience on a whole new scale. Independence on a whole new scale.

We felt this purpose (and a gratitude for it) far more deeply there as spirits than we can ever recreate or relate to here as physical beings. Earth life was to be a mission so intense, so varied, so eternity-changing that we may not have comprehended it fully. Part of the purpose was to "link" us to each other in ways far more intimate than we had yet experienced. We would come as helpless babies, completely dependent on our parents—parents who would then, through this remarkable new concept of time and aging, eventually become dependent on us. At death, each of us (including those who died without having all of the experiences, all of the relationships, all of the choices and commitments they needed) would pass on to a new kind of spiritual place where, with the memory of our physical lives intact, much of the learning could continue. From there, through our own ongoing experience, through observing this earth, and through the vicarious experience of those still on earth (particularly our descendants), we would continue to learn and develop and make choices as we awaited a great culmination and resurrection when spirit and perfected body would reunite as a more completed and more joyful soul.

The scope and wonder and beauty of God's plan and our purpose was stunning. A level of growth and life had been opened to us that manifested the completeness and immensity of God's love. He was willing to literally give us everything He had—to let us try to experience and become all that He had. We realized, there in the remarkable light of that plan, that there were no limits to God's love.

Opposition, Risk, and the Answer

The mortality plan was not without opposition. There were those who wanted less risk. They were led by a dark and demanding prince with his own agenda and a lust for power. He instilled fear by questioning the plan and our ability to participate successfully in it. If we left, how could we return? Freedom of choice encompassed the possibility of failure—indeed, the virtual guarantee of wrong choices in some things. Would our bad decisions, our failures, our errors prevent us from making it back to God's presence and God's family? We understood that the price for the knowledge of mortal experience could be the loss of the very innocence that allowed us to live with God.

You and I may have been perplexed, but we were not persuaded by the opposition. We understood that without freedom and the risk it implied, the powerful purposes of mortality could not be fully realized or the godlike rewards fully obtained.

Despite the power of what our spirits had felt in learning of God's plan for mortality, the most magnificent moment and the deepest emotion were yet to come. Both came as the missing piece in the puzzle of the plan—as the overwhelming answer to our fearful question about how we could return. They came when one who was with God and who was God made a condescension beyond imagination, offering to sacrifice Himself in a way that would bridge the chasm between God's realm and where we would find ourselves after our plunge into mortality. Using His own perfection as the ultimate collateral, He offered to pay our debts, to undergo the collective pain of all, and to somehow absorb and atone for all error and sin, making it possible for each of us to return. He offered to use His bounty to pay for our folly, His infinite perfection to compensate for our countless mistakes. He offered to do so at a price of pain beyond calculation or imagination.

The feelings unlocked in us by that condescension went beyond anything we had ever known. The generosity and power of the offered atonement filled us with awe. He who owed us nothing would give us everything. At the cost of unimaginable personal suffering, He would use his endless credits to balance our endless debits. He would give himself as a ransom in the ultimate act of love.

The Creation

This earth was created not out of nothing but out of matter that already existed and was brought together and organized. The time it took and the methods that were used are not comprehensible to us here, but it was a natural process, governed by higher laws, some known only to God. The earth was formed and beautified and populated with a vast array of life. There, then, we were aware of the framing of this incredible earth. Here, now, the details of that creation are above and far beyond our finite minds. There, we lived in a realm of eternity, where time was not relevant, and we lived with God, whose ways and powers were infinite. Here, we live in finite, time-bound mortality where the *how* and *when* questions are too far beyond us to be relevant.

What is relevant is the *why* question. The *reason* for the earth was *us*, the spirit children of God. The earth with all its wonders was made for us—a gift of immense and eternal proportions. It was created by power and methods surpassing our time and comprehension, and when it was ready, we began taking our turns in mortality.

When those turns came, and what they consisted of, was part of God's plan. Just as different children in our families today may need different schools according to their unique, individual abilities and needs (and their own unique weaknesses), so each of us needed different circumstances and challenges during our physical lives to maximize our opportunity for growth and progression. Thus what may look arbitrary and unfair in terms of where and how people come into the world is, to God with His ultimate perspective, exactly what is potentially and ultimately best for each of us.

So to this world you came, taking your turn, coming into the body and the time and the circumstances that God willed for you. Your physical body was conceived by your parents, and you were born on earth. The veil of spiritual forgetfulness dropped across your mind, and you grew from a baby. Within you is your spirit, the essence of who you are and have always been. Beyond you lies the potential and possibility of returning to God and bringing with you all that you have learned and all that you have become while here. You are alone but not alone. God is accessible by prayer, and your spirit is accessible simply by the acknowledgment that it is there.

Thus you are related to every person on this earth who lives, who has lived, who will yet live. Physically you might be my distant cousin, one hundred or one thousand times removed, but spiritually you are my sibling. There is purpose in this earth and in everything that happens here—purpose and plan. You are part of that plan, as am I, and the plan is of and from a real and personal God who sent us here from a life before life.

Waiting and Watching

As you waited for your turn on earth, you were not unaware of mortality or of those who descended into it before you did. On the contrary, you were vitally interested in those whose lives preceded yours, particularly in those you had known and associated with and in those who would be your ancestors on earth.

My great-grandfather was an immigrant to the United States from a tiny village in Sweden. When I first visited the home and farm where he grew up, it was hauntingly familiar. It was a sunny summer day, and I walked into the pine trees behind the old house and lay down on the thick, spongy moss that covered the forest floor. My mind wandered, and I realized that I was, that very year, the same age he had been when he left home and country to seek a new life in America. What I felt was more memory than history. I had watched this man. I knew him. He was part of me.

The memory slivers came home from Sweden with me and surfaced at random times. When I got involved in building an addition on our house, certain tools felt warmly familiar in my hands—he was a carpenter. When I first strapped on cross-country skis, the sport came remarkably naturally to me—it had been his primary form of transportation six months of the year.

We may not have been able (or even inclined) to see all that went on on this earth from our spiritual existence. But there were some times and some people in which and in whom we had particular personal interest. We were aware of certain individual spirits—of their lives on earth and of some particular experiences they were having.

Though our interest and anticipation was high, we were happy to wait for our own individual mortal turns. We knew that the time in which we would come—a later time—would be filled with exceptional opportunity, options, and possibility. We were content to continue with life as we knew it there and to wait for life as we would come to know it here.

Happiness

Any loving parent wants one ultimate thing for his or her children—happiness. We may have all kinds of other hopes and dreams for our offspring—a good education, a happy marriage, sound health, a productive career—but all are means-to-an-end objectives. The ultimate goal is happiness.

It is the same, only vastly and perfectly complete, with God. His purpose is our happiness. In the premortal life, we understood this purpose with a clarity and surety that are beyond us here, and thus we were awed and overwhelmed by God's wondrous mortal plan to bring this purpose about. We knew this plan, we understood it, we chose to participate in it.

God's "mortality plan" for the salvation and progression of us, His children, was perfect and complete . . . and *new*. It involved a host of elements never before experienced: earth and bodies, families and parental love, romance and relationships, service and joy, time and progression. Each of these new elements, and our premortal perception of them, deserves further attention because each is necessary for our ultimate happiness. . . .

Earth and Bodies

The ferns in the forests, the evening hues and shadows of deep canyons, the black, starry desert sky, the thundering ocean surf . . . the earth surrounds us with beauty and also teaches of

God. Our bodies interact with the earth—sensing it, using it, learning from it. Our bodies themselves educate our spirits through experiences and encounters with pain and pleasure, exhilaration and exhaustion, sensation and suffering. God's plan called for leaving the controlled, predictable greenhouse environment of a spirit world and plunging into the chaotic unpredictability of physical mortality.

Our bodies afford us the joys of passion and of discipline. Our appetites, from food to sex, offer us experience and pleasure our spirits had never known, and the agency that allows appetites to destroy some people allows others to learn the discipline that upgrades pleasure to joy.

The mortal bodies promised us in premortal life and given to us here are the beginning step of the completion of our souls. Never mind that our bodies now are subject to all manner of problem and pain. They are in the image of the complete God, and they will ultimately, after teaching us through their imperfections, become perfected in the resurrection and allow us to know more of what God knows. Our specific bodies, with their particular infirmities and frailties, are the very bodies we each need to maximize our individual opportunities to overcome, to experience, and to grow.

Babies, capable of infusing us with a uniquely tender form of love, are the creation and design of God, who prepared a way for an adult spirit to develop a body. In the purity of little children, we see God.

Families and Parental Love

Before I was a parent, the idea of being willing to give my life for someone was beyond my comprehension. One night, looking at our firstborn toddler as she slept, I realized how quickly and how easily I would die for her if the choice were her or me.

As parents, we reach levels of unconditional love that are otherwise impossible. And other kinds of new levels are reached through romantic and marital love. These levels of love and interdependence were and are a part of the plan we knew and rejoiced in during our premortal life.

Family is the organization of God—one of generations rather than governments, of patriarchy rather than politics.

The joy we felt in the life before life was not an isolated or individualistic happiness. It was communal. We were to become linked and interdependent in a most remarkable and real way. We were to be children and descendants of some of our spiritual siblings, and parents and progenitors of others.

The worship of ancestors was not a part of this plan, but the respect and reverence of them was, as was the cherishing and stewardship of children. This sentiment is stated in the words of the last verse of the Old Testament, which speaks of the turning of "the heart of the fathers to the children, and the heart of the children to their fathers." This turning, collectively, can save our society. Individually, it can save our souls.

New Dimensions of Love

Love was certainly not unknown to us in our premortal life. We loved God with a love that combined deep personal feelings toward a father with worshipful awe toward a Creator. And we felt a spiritual version of sibling love for each other—particularly for those we knew and associated with. But romantic love and parental love and some other kinds of family and personal relationships are new to us in mortality and are part of the reason for our physical lives.

This expansion of love is one profound purpose of mortality. My father, who died of cancer when I was fifteen but whose spirit and influence I continue to feel, understood this. In a letter he wrote to me the day before he died, he told me to learn how to love. He wrote that when one truly loves, everything else takes care of itself. I've come to feel (partly, I believe, through his ongoing promptings) that God, who loves so completely that He *is* love, sent us here to learn to love more, to experience new kinds and new dimensions of love.

Most people who have faith in an afterlife believe that these new and deepest loves, their fondest relationships, can endure death—that they will still love and be with those they love in the next life. The new kinds of love we learn here go with us and expand our souls in the life to come.

Service and Joy

Many parents have discovered that children learn more about love by serving than by being served. One Christmas we decided as a family to forego the usual gifts and frantic festivity and to use the money saved to go on a humanitarian expedition to Bolivia, where we helped lay pipe to bring water to a primitive Andean village. I'll never forget the love on our twelve-year-old daughter's face as the village children turned on the completed connection and saw the magical arrival of water that they had always had to carry. Dusty and exhausted, our daughter said, "This is the best Christmas present I've ever had."

In our life before life we had none of the physical *needs* or problems that we have now, first, because we were spirits, and second, because we were with God. When there are no needs, there is no service. And when there is no service, a great and particular type of joy cannot exist.

The joy of serving, of helping, of recognizing and meeting the needs of others was part of the plan for our mortality. Here, we realized, there would be endless needs. The problems, challenges, and difficulties of a physical life would cause us to need each other and would afford us countless chances to give. Giving, a godlike process, would produce joy for both the giver and the receiver.

We usually love those who serve us, and we always, over time, love those whom we serve. In our life before life we realized that love itself, the greatest godlike quality, would be fostered and expanded by our mortal lives on earth.

Time and Progression

We've all experienced having the intention to do something but having no time frame in which to do it—no deadline. Such things rarely get done. On a much vaster scale, we can try to imagine making progress and accomplishing change in an eternal environment where there literally was no time. Within an existence completely open-ended, certain types of growth and progress were extremely difficult and limited. By giving us a finite lifetime in a structured physical world with measurable years, days, and hours, God's plan gave us opportunities for a new kind of progress.

As we stood there in our premortality, on the brink of time, we understood far more than we can now about the *gift* of time. On earth, we would learn to work and function within time, to do mental and physical work within time frames, to set deadlines, and to bring things to pass. It would be a new, accelerated kind of progression, like a focal point on an eternal, blurred line or a tiny knot in an endless thread.

We can enhance the joy of this tiny knot or focal point of time by being aware of the thread going forever forward and forever backward. We can know there is a life after and a life before, but we can also remember what the Sanskrit poet said: "Today, well lived, makes every yesterday a dream of joy and every tomorrow a vision of hope."

As each of us was assigned a time in the sequence of mortality, those of us who are here now received the blessing of coming late in that sequence, at a time when options and awareness are far greater than in earlier times. Whatever it was that qualified us for this, we should be profoundly grateful.

Answers for Mortality

❦ ❦ ❦ ❦ ❦

Why it helps to know (what changes when we do)

If . . . Then

Mortality is the pivotally important physical place between spiritual past and spiritual future. How it is designed for each of us was determined by our past existence. Knowledge of that past can influence how we live our present, which in turn determines our future eternity.

Focus on the first part of that last sentence. How can knowledge of or belief in a prelife influence how we live here and now? What difference can it make in terms of who we are and where we are going with our lives? Answer these questions by imagining an orphan without home or heritage. There are no expectations and no encouragement; he lives only for and only with himself. Then one day he finds his parents, his family, and his past (or they find him). Suddenly he knows he was not a product of chance or of abandonment as he had assumed. He learns that he was taken from his family at birth and thus has no memory of his infancy with them. But now he has found them, and they are a strong and honorable family—they have missed him, longed for him, and they love him deeply.

What changes? Everything changes: his perspective, his self-image, his confidence. He gains hope and home and heritage and thus a deep sense of worth. He overcomes loneliness and the listless lethargy of the lost. His new knowledge of his past, where he came from and who he really is, dramatically alters his present and his future.

Belief in our *spiritual* past can have an even more profound effect.

Ponder first a list of the insights offered in the previous chapters; then contemplate a second list—of how we (and our lives) are changed by these insights. Please read the second list slowly, pondering and focusing on the significance of each potential life change.

If we can believe that we are . . .

1. spiritual beings who came from and will return to a spiritual place,

2. offspring of God with the mortal purpose of experience and expansion,

3. spirits who were loyal to God's plan for our mortality and who agreed to come to this earth to fulfill that plan,

4. spiritual children who become physical parents to

spiritual siblings, learning through families the deepest lessons of love,

5. somewhat chosen or favored spirits to live in this late time of maximal options and opportunities, and

6. benefactors of an atonement that allows us to overcome mistakes and return to God . . .

Then, because of these beliefs:

1. We can live within a longer-term framework with broader goals and perspectives.

2. We can make better decisions, basing them on the longest-term (lifetime) goal of *returning* to our eternal home.

3. We can accept illnesses, accidents, and crises as temporary challenges and opportunities for learning.

4. We can have deeper faith that God, in His eternal perspective, is loving, wise, and fair rather than arbitrary or capricious.

5. We can see marriage (and our marriage partners) in a completely new, respectful, and eternal perspective.

6. We can understand our children much better and grasp why they are so different from us (and from their brothers or sisters). We can respect our children more and understand that

the generations could have been reversed and that, if not for birth order, *they* could have been *our* parents.

7. We can prioritize and balance our lives more effectively, with more emphasis on what lasts longest—the relationships and self-worth that predate and postdate this world.

8. We can have a paradigm of stewardship, which breeds appreciation and awareness, rather than a paradigm of ownership, which breeds either envy and jealousy or pride and conceit.

9. We can hope more for spiritual guidance in the events of our lives and less for physical control over all of them.

10. We can accept our dependence on God and interdependence with people rather than seeking independence from both.

11. We can have better, deeper reasons for day-to-day goodness and day-to-day joy.

12. We can develop and feel a new and more real kind of gratitude, which enhances happiness regardless of our circumstances.

13. We can develop a unique combination of humility and

confidence, with both stemming from our eternal relationship to a loving and perfect Heavenly Father.

14. We can learn to see our talents, gifts, and favorable circumstances not as privileges but as responsibilities—as opportunities and obligations to help others and serve the God who gave them all to us.

15. We can love our spiritual brothers and sisters (everyone) more and eliminate prejudice, intolerance, nationalism, and other related poisons from our lives.

16. We can find deeper appreciation for nature and for the beauty of the earth as literal gifts from God.

17. We can form a more real relationship with God and thus pray more insightfully and appreciate the atonement more knowledgeably.

18. We can deal with questions of creation, realizing that understanding God's motives is more important and more possible than understanding His methods.

19. We can view ourselves with greater respect and higher regard, knowing that our physical weaknesses and appetites can ultimately be overcome by our spiritual potential.

20. We can look at the hereafter not as a vague or mythical

place of eternal rest but as a continuing phase of eternal progress.

Benefits of a Belief in a Before

Note that each of the twenty benefits just listed begins with "we can." Belief in a life before life is an *enabler*. It allows us to understand things and to do things that are beyond the capacity of one who thinks back only to birth. Each of the twenty deserves a deeper look. They have not been listed (or now explained) in any particular order of importance because, when we think of them, each one is of ultimate importance. They are numbered only to make it easier to keep track of them and relate each to the preceding list.

1. Broader Framework

Time-management and goal-setting experts tell us that the best short-term goals are derived and divided from clear long-term goals. People who have planned their month are more clear about what they want to do each week or each day.

Likewise, setting goals and priorities for life works better when we know something of eternity and its purposes.

As mentioned earlier, in my consulting firm, I've sat with businesspeople as they have tried to carve out their mission statements, their pro forma projections, their short- and long-term corporate goals. I find they can always be far more insightful in looking at their future if they remember their past. I encourage them to think a little about where they have come from and why they joined a company in the first place. Within that perspective, goals for the future become more meaningful and more clear.

We came to this earth to progress, to learn to control the physical, to make choices and face challenges, to love, to have families and deepen relationships. If we set goals based on where we came from and why we are here, we will find more joy in this physical present and more connection to our spiritual future.

2. Better Decisions

Not only the goals we set but the decisions we make are strengthened and simplified by a knowledge of where we came from. The word *return* can become a one-word mission statement that incorporates an understanding of our spiritual past and future and a recognition of purpose here in between. A deep desire to fulfill mortality's purpose, to live and learn and love in such a way that we are worthy to return to God ... such a mindset can influence every decision we make, large or small.

In the Eyre family, each child has a chart in the privacy of the last page of his or her diary or journal labeled "Decisions in Advance." The idea is that if we know where we came from and why we are here, many decisions, even ones we are years away from implementing, become more simple and clear. Our children have made such entries as these: "I will not do drugs," "I will be honest," "I will save sex for married commitment and love," "I will graduate from college." The best long-term future decisions are made with a view toward our long-term past and our long-term purpose.

3. Crisis as Opportunity

I met a blind man years ago on a street corner in Southampton on the south coast of England. He and his seeing-eye dog were selling baskets. In our brief conversation he taught me much about humor and about perspective.

"Did you make the baskets?" I asked.

"All but the dog baskets. The dog made those."

As we talked, he detected a trace of pity in my voice and he didn't like it. "See here," he said, "you've got one sense that works better than mine, but I've got four that work better than yours." He then proved it by telling me of sounds I could not hear and smells I could not smell. He said he thought of his blindness as an opportunity that had opened whole worlds to him.

That perspective would come more easily to all of us if we could accept that we came from and will return to a place without physical infirmity, and that such challenges (indeed all challenges) are part of the purpose for our being here. Faith in both our spiritual past and our spiritual future won't take the pain out of illness, injury, and personal loss, but it will lend a degree of faith and scope to our hardest times and allow us to accept them as part of a plan we agreed to long ago.

4. A Wise and Fair God

If you walked into a stadium in the middle of a race, you wouldn't declare the race unfair because some runners were ahead of others. You wouldn't call the race organizer unfeeling or arbitrary and refuse to support or believe in him. You would assume that the runners who were ahead got there by their earlier efforts and, if you were a knowledgeable race fan, you would also assume that some of the runners now behind would end up ahead. And you would understand that each runner runs his own race in his own way for his own reasons.

Perhaps an even better metaphor is the story of an Australian aborigine going on an extended "walkabout" from his primitive tribe and by chance returning on the day that a medical missionary, who arrived in his absence, is performing an appendectomy on his wife. What the aborigine sees is a white man using a sharp knife to cut into his wife. All of the conclusions that jump to his mind are wrong.

Just as wrong are the judgments people make in viewing this world. They see some rich and some poor; some crippled and some healthy; some living long and well in wickedness and others, good and earnest, dying young—and they conclude either that there is no God or that God is uninterested or unfair.

If the aborigine knew the full story, he would thank the doctor. If we knew the full spectrum of opportunity we would thank God for giving each of us the circumstances and the challenges that maximize our opportunity for growth, learning, and progress.

5. Eternal Partners

A partnership of convenience." "Something we'll try, to see if it works." "A conditional commitment." "A good thing until one or both of us changes and moves on." So many of today's definitions or perceptions of marriage are just that shallow and temporary. Marriages become flighty and fragile, and when they break they leave behind so much hurt and often so much damage to children.

What could fix them? What could make them stronger? In simple terms, *a longer-term perspective*. We can know we were sent here as members of God's family to form eternal families of our own, understanding that the commitments and deeper levels of love involved in marriage are central and critical to our purpose in being here. Working through marital difficulties and adjusting together constitute the very kind of emotional and spiritual maturing that God expects of us here—that He sent us here to gain.

Freedom of choice is what allows us to grow and progress while we are here. But we must remember that our physical lives are short, and if we make short-term choices of convenience, moving in and out of relationships rather than staying committed and working through problems, we will have little to take with us when we leave this life.

Two people who believe that they can remain together and committed after this life can develop a depth or "oneness" that is otherwise impossible. They can interact with a spiritual synergy that can change their world.

6. Children, Brothers, Sisters, and Parents

My five-year-old daughter said something unconsciously profound one lazy Sunday afternoon. She marched up to me, looked me straight in the eye, and said, "You're not really my daddy." Having instantly captured my full attention, she explained, "In Sunday School my teacher said that God is our Father and we're all brothers and sisters."

I relaxed for a minute, but she wasn't finished. "And I've been thinking about it, Dad, and I think I'm really your big sister."

In her mind it might have been a child's demand for more respect. But to me, knowing the specialness of her spirit and believing in a life before, it was a statement of probability.

Whatever the case, I know that my belief that we both lived before in a spiritual place makes me respect her more. It makes me more aware of the trust she put in me by coming to me as a helpless infant. It makes me try harder to repay her trust by being the best dad I can be.

Knowing of a life before life helps us see that our children are who they are—that they are each unique and need individually tailored parenting from us. Children are not "lumps of clay" that "parent sculptors" can mold into whatever they wish. They are more like seedlings, looking similar to each other in their infancy but each programmed to become its own unique kind of tree. We parents are gardeners, and we do best if we *observe* what "kind" each child is and try to nurture accordingly.

Knowing of a life before life also helps us to understand why our children are so different from each other and to blame ourselves less for some of our children's less desirable tendencies even as we try harder to help them overcome.

Perhaps the most important thing parents can do is *watch*

and *observe* their children, striving to know who they truly are—their unique and inherent gifts, inclinations, talents, and personalities. One of the worst things parents can do, on the other hand, is try to force kids into being something the parents wish for, without regard to who and what the child already is.

Some children have gifts and propensities so obvious and so profound that it is only natural to help them develop those. And it is also only natural to believe that they developed those talents before this life. How *unnatural* to believe, for example, that Mozart's virtuosity was just a product of chance. Most children's gifts and natures are more subtle than Mozart's and take longer to flower and longer to recognize. Still, any parent who stares into an infant's eyes begins to sense that that child came from somewhere else and brought a lot into this life. Focusing on and responding to that feeling can make us better parents.

7. Priorities and Balance

Y ou can't take it with you." The old cliché is supposed to motivate us *away* from materialism and from things that have no eternal significance. How about a positive corollary that can motivate us *toward* the things of real value:

"You brought it with you to build on and take back with you."

We brought with us, within our spirits, such things as our characters, our personalities, our talents and gifts, our relationship with God. Mortality, with its enhanced experience and options, allows us to build on all those eternal things and to return with them intact—deepened and expanded.

This knowledge can have powerful impact on our priorities, causing us to take more time for family, for friends, and for self-development and helping us avoid the obsessions with career and material things that destroy our balance.

8. Stewardship Paradigm

If we think of an "ownership attitude" metaphorically as a tree trunk, what are the branches growing out? When we see someone who owns more, we grow limbs of envy or jealousy or resentment. When we see those with less, we sprout branches of conceit or pride.

Ownership is certainly a viable economic concept, but as a spiritual paradigm it is poison. "All I want is the property next to mine" is an insatiable appetite that takes our time and energy away from more important things.

Belief in a Creator who made this earth for us to live on and enjoy can change our paradigm to "stewardship." From the stewardship perspective, the earth and everything in it and on it belong to God, and the best parts are free for us to use. On the attitude trunk of stewardship grow branches of sharing, empathy, tolerance, and charity. Ownership's pressure is replaced by stewardship's pleasure; stress yields to serenity, competition to cooperation.

9. Guidance Rather Than Control

I had a professor at the Harvard Business School whose mantra was, "Act, don't react! Always be in control. If you lose control it is because you didn't do sufficient contingency planning."

I found, in the real world, that his approach led to more frustration than fulfillment. I learned how preposterous (and how presumptuous) it is to think we can or should control all circumstances, situations, and other people.

Control of self and of appetites *is* possible, and it is a big part of why we are here, but in this interactive, spontaneous, and surprising world, *reacting* well is as important as *acting*, and most everything *but* ourselves is largely beyond our control.

When we realize that we came from God and that everything around us is His, we get a release from the compulsion to control. We work to be our best selves, but we also accept and trust what comes to us—either as opportunity or as challenge. We look for answers through prayer, and we understand that promptings and guidance from One who knows all are worth more than pseudo attempts at control by those (ourselves included) who know next to nothing.

10. Dependence and Interdependence

If you take a stroll through the self-help section of a bookstore, you may be overwhelmed by the number of titles on financial independence, emotional independence, and the "freedom" of not needing others.

Again, the notions of rugged individualism, self-reliance, and independence are great economic principles but inappropriate spiritual ones. The ideal of not needing anyone doesn't work when dealing with God and with our spirits. It is not independence but acknowledged dependence on God that brings true peace and strength. And happiness has more to do with our interdependence with other people than our independence from them.

All this becomes far easier to understand in the light of a prelife where all of us were members of God's family. We came here to learn to think and act with a degree of self-reliance and independence, but not to *not need* God or others. Knowing our ultimate complete dependence on God makes "self-help" an oxymoron. And knowing where we came from can help us to appreciate the eternal connections between us all . . . and to spiritually seek interdependence and synergy rather than independence and self-sufficiency.

11. Day-to-Day Goodness and Day-to-Day Joy

E at, drink, and be merry, for tomorrow we die" is all too descriptive of how many of us live our lives. The "no tomorrow" paradigm produces a hedonistic mentality that leads to all sorts of bad short-term decisions. Those choices in turn affect the long term and the very long term, which is a reality whether we like it or not.

What a different life we lead if our motto is, "Become all you can be and give all you can give, for tomorrow we *return* to the God who sent us here." This believing mentality not only changes our "eating and drinking" (how we approach and handle every appetite) but it advances the notion of "being merry" from the grasping of short-term pleasure to the building of long-term joy.

The two ways of thinking are polar opposites. In the "no tomorrow" mindset, we satisfy our appetites. In the "return" mindset, we control our appetites. With "no tomorrow," the law of the jungle makes sense; with "return," the laws of God make sense.

The choice is pleasure versus joy, with *pleasure* defined as "if it feels good, do it" and *joy* defined as long-term relationships and commitments and a genuine caring for the needs and feelings of others. Actually, in the spiritual "return" paradigm, even the hedonistic law can turn good: "If it feels good *to your spirit*, do it." Spiritually it feels good to discipline ourselves, to sacrifice for others, to be honest and committed and true.

Remember that while mortality with all its choices is a test, the goal or purpose of the test is joy. In the context of the "return" paradigm, God's commandments are *loving counsel from a wise Father.* He knows the ingredients and the makeup of true and lasting joy, and He gives us that formula through His laws and commandments, along with a world that is filled with opportunities for the joy He sent us here to find.

I have a wonderful old friend, a rural country doctor, who shares my convictions about a life before life. I love to go on road trips with him and talk about life and ideas and philosophy. On one such drive he asked me, "What do you think will be God's first question to you on judgment day?" I surmised that it would have something to do with how well I'd done keeping God's commandments. "I doubt it," he said. "I think the first question will be about the goal, not about the plan. The commandments are His plan, His way. The goal—His goal for us—is *joy*. I think He'll want to know how much joy we found down here. He'll say, 'How much did you enjoy those mountains I made for you, or those seacoasts, or those sunsets? How much joy did you have in your marriage and your family? How much joy did you give others?'"

If God made the world for our joy, then the most important measurement of our accomplishments here is how much real joy we found. Did we figure out that His commandments were a plan for maximizing our joy? Did we live that plan? Did we find the joy?

12. Happiness-Enhancing Gratitude

It has been said that the amount of happiness we feel is exactly and directly proportionate to how much gratitude we feel.

The problem, then, with taking too much credit ourselves for what we do or what we have is that it cuts down on the gratitude we feel to someone else and thus cuts down happiness.

True gratitude can't exist in the abstract. It needs a *receiver*—someone to give the gratitude to. Our greatest gifts come from God, and when we recognize Him as our spiritual Father who sent us here, our gratitude becomes real and specific and meaningful.

The Eyres have a Thanksgiving Day tradition of sitting down as the turkey cooks and making lists of what we are especially thankful for that year. This past Thanksgiving, twenty-three of us—children, cousins, uncles, and aunts—each made a personal "thankful list" of fifty things and then read them to each other. As I listened, two things amazed me. The first was how few duplications there were. With twenty-three of us each listing fifty, there were 1,150 "thankful things," and except for a few predictable overlaps like "family," "faith," and "friends," almost every one was thought of and mentioned by only one person. Conclusion: There are an unbelievable number of things to be thankful for. The second surprise to me was how many of the "thankful things" were gifts of this earth, this mortality. Mountains, oceans, eyes, ears, experiences of all kinds, trials to overcome, challenges met, places visited . . . hundreds of things brought happiness, all part of our unique mortal experience on this earth, all impossible without it. Conclusion: This earth, this mortality truly was created for our joy.

As I listened to the "thankful things," to the joy conveyed by each, I thought back again to my narrowly reopened memory of our spiritual life before life and our reaction to God's plan of a physical earth experience. We *shouted for joy* at the prospect of these experiences and possibilities. We sensed, looking forward, how joyful they would be.

Now, looking back, we can focus on and enhance that gratitude.

13. *"Confident Humility"*

It sounds like another oxymoron—a combination of two opposites. Yet, with a belief in a life before life, the words *confidence* and *humility* work together and complement each other.

We are confident because we come from God, as His spirit children. What could give more confidence than that lineage, the spiritual genetics of a perfect and all-knowing Father?

Our humility then has the same source. God's perfection provides the ultimate contrast to our weakness, frailty, and dependence on Him.

Thus we are confident because of our relationship to God and we are humble because of our relationship to God. And the combination—a humble confidence or a confident humility—is perhaps the most attractive and the most desirable of all human qualities.

14. *Gifts, Opportunities, and Obligations*

The attitude of "I earned it, I own it, and I'm privileged because of it" is completely stripped away by belief in a prelife and in a God who gave us our bodies, our earth, and our circumstances. Of course some seem to make more of their lives than others. But they are building on and with the raw materials given by God. And knowing that we each came with unique challenges designed for us by God can allow us to look at others with respect and empathy and to see our blessings not as prideful privileges but as opportune obligations to become all we can be and to give all we can give.

The attitude, in this light, changes to "I was given it, God owns it, and I'm blessed and able to share because of it."

15. Antidotes to the Poison of Prejudice

A close associate of mine years ago was an astronaut who had the remarkable experience of orbiting the earth in the space shuttle. One of the things he told me—something that made a powerful impression on him as he looked down on the earth—was that there are no *boundaries*. You don't see countries or races or religions from up there. You see one beautiful and undivided earth, and you realize that we create our own boundaries and divide ourselves out of ignorance.

We can enjoy the same perspective—perhaps even to a greater degree—by figuratively looking down at this earth from a belief in a life before life. The fact that we all came from the same place, from the same parents, with the same purpose is far stronger as a "uniter" than any difference or prejudice can be as a "divider." We obtain true and lasting tolerance when we understand that our eternal spiritual commonality completely overwhelms any temporary, temporal differences.

In this light, prejudice, nationalism, racism, and any notion of intolerance or superiority become foolishness—poisons to our spirits that we avoid like plagues.

16. Alignment with Nature

It is one thing to recognize beauty in the earth, to acknowledge our special affinity with nature and the natural world. But it is another thing, and deeply and richly satisfying, to see the earth as a remarkable and inexhaustible gift from God, an orbiting laboratory and school expressly created to facilitate our learning, our continued progression, and our joy.

In this perspective, nature and the earth itself become vehicles for knowing God. The glory of a sunrise, the perfect hues and color schemes of a landscape, the majesty of a mountain, the power of the ocean's currents and tides, the serenity of an old forest, all become witnesses of God and indicators of His nature as well as of His love for us.

Although anyone who believes in God can enjoy a deep gratitude in this perspective, one with a belief in life before life with God can feel it more deeply and understand the earth's purpose more purely.

17. Relationships with God

At the university one of our children attended, there was a young woman from another country who was being "sponsored" by a benefactor she had never met. She wrote often to this man, telling him of her progress in school and always thanking him. And he wrote back, encouraging her. She hoped, after the completion of her education, to meet him personally.

Believers in God who have no faith in or knowledge of a life before life are in a similar situation. They are grateful to God. They may communicate with Him and thank Him through prayer, but they look forward to (or fear) meeting Him for the first time. Such a relationship can never be quite the same as an *ongoing* one, comparable to that of a student who is sent away to school by loving parents with plans and hopes of *returning*. Such a student, even if he forgets much of his home and earlier life, still can rekindle and feel the love of his parents and appreciate their support and their wisdom in sending him to school.

Knowing we lived with and came from God can intensify our love for Him and promote our acceptance of His love for us. And understanding that One, in our premortal presence, volunteered His own sacrifice to make possible our return can fill our hearts with devotion and provide the strongest motivation of all to live as He asked us to live.

18. *Motives, Not Methods*

Perhaps through all the science in this world and all that human beings may yet discover via exploration and experimentation, we will learn some tiny fraction of *how* this world and this universe came to be. But what we do know of the "how" will always be dwarfed by what we don't know. Indeed, many scientists say that any small increase they gain in *knowing* geometrically increases how much they know that they *don't know*.

And though probing the "how" will always intrigue us (and

educate us), it is the "why" that will help us most and that is most accessible to our spirits.

Spirituality and religion in their truest forms always deal more with the why than with the how. God makes little effort to tell us how He created this world, doubtless because our finite minds are incapable of understanding His infinite intelligence. But He does tell us why—because knowledge of purpose is helpful (if not essential) to the fulfilling of purpose. The earth was created for a purpose—to facilitate God's marvelous plan for the progress of His children.

How that creation occurred, what methods were used, how long it took, what parts of the earth were organized from materials that existed elsewhere—these and a million other "how" questions are interesting, but not as essential or as answerable as the question of "why." Many of the how questions may be completely irrelevant in a creation that occurred outside the limits of time and law and space as we know them.

True faith comes when we trust that God's *methods* are beyond us but that His *motives* are for us. We can then quit worrying about the former and start wondering (as in "the wonder of it all") about the latter.

19. Loving and Being Gentle with Yourself

I once wrote a book titled *I Challenge You/I Promise You*, which laid out thirty spiritual challenges and gave some suggestions for meeting them. I've had more feedback (and gratitude expressed) about one of those challenges than about the other twenty-nine added together. It was the challenge to "be gentle with yourself," and it simply involved self-respect and the realization that God knows of our weaknesses, loves us completely in spite of them, and put us here on earth so we would have enhanced opportunities to overcome them. He doesn't expect our perfection, at least not here on this earth. He just expects effort and faith.

Knowing that we are God's spiritual children and that we lived with Him in a life before life can increase our regard and our respect for ourselves. It can give us faith that, over time, the goodness of our spirits can turn our weaknesses into strengths. That perspective can make us more patient and more gentle with ourselves.

I remember hearing an apology once that deeply impressed me. It was a public apology by an elected official who had broken the public trust. With honest regret he said, "That was not my truest self."

Most of us know, in our more introspective moments, that our deepest, truest selves are noble and good. We are natural, physical people with countless faults, weaknesses, lusts, and appetites, and we are prone toward all kinds of mistakes. Yet, deep down, our core is good.

Believing that, reminding ourselves of that, not only helps us feel better about ourselves but helps us become better people. And when the notion is backed up and made specific by a belief in a life before life, we begin to feel a genuine self-worth that supersedes all of our self-doubt and weakness.

This belief in an eternal self that is inherently good and that came from God is worth infinitely more than the temporary pump-ups of self-help and pop psychology. We certainly can try to motivate ourselves by looking in the mirror and repeating, "Every day, in every way, I'm getting better and better." But something always reminds us of our failures and flaws. It's a different story to believe that underneath our mistakes and within our weakness-prone physical selves is an eternal spirit from a higher, better place—a spirit that has both a purpose and a destiny. In this frame, our growth, improvement, and happiness relate not so much to temporary self-motivation about who we can become as to a deep spiritual remembering of who we already are.

20. Loving the Here but Relishing the Herebefore and Looking Forward to the Hereafter

Some of the general religious ideas concerning the hereafter, perhaps intended just as metaphors or symbols, can be a bit unnerving, if not downright discouraging. Pictures of hell as a torturing inferno or of heaven as a harp-playing endless rest on fluffy clouds seem almost equally unrealistic and equally unappealing. And perhaps even more disturbing is some imaginary line that qualifies us for one or the other. Somewhere in the middle part of the infinite scale between the best life and the worst life there must be two people, as close to identical as you can get, where one just makes it and goes to harp heaven and the other just misses and goes to hot hell.

Few believe literally in this symbolic simplicity, yet most people do believe in life after life. The concept of an afterlife begins to take on a sense of reality when it is *connected* to prelife, when we see it (as well as this life) as an ongoing phase of our progression and development. What we did before affects us here and now, and what we do now affects us there and then. All of life is real, and our spirits have a real past and a real future.

Even in the limited mortal or physical context, the happiest and most interesting people are those who have learned the balance of living in the past *and* the present *and* the future. They enjoy reflection and memories of childhood and earlier times (diaries, family videos, scrapbooks). They plan and anticipate and look forward to the future (goals, mission statements, planning calendars). And they appreciate the present, relishing every experience, whether expected or a surprise.

The same three-pronged perspective can exist spiritually. We ponder and pray and seek faith concerning a prelife and thus gain insight that creates joy in our sense of who we are and where we came from. We believe and look forward to an afterlife in which our awareness will expand and our progress will continue. And, in between, we appreciate our marvelous physical *present*, in which we are the recipients of so many marvelous gifts of God.

Conscious
Application

❦ ❦ ❦ ❦ ❦

Using the insight to change your life (and your world)

Changing How We Think and Live

The insights or perspectives that life before life opens to us are as valuable or as worthless as we choose to make them. It is what we *do* with them and about them that determines their true value. Beyond what we believe, we must consciously change *how* we think about ourselves, about others, and about our day-to-day lives.

How can the insights of a premortal life be consciously applied to daily life—to our goals, to our relationships, to our careers, to the people we encounter and associate with, to how we live each day? Powerful as these new perspectives and insights are, they need individual implementation if they are to truly change our lives.

The world around us will not support or reinforce our eternal spiritual paradigm. The clamor and chaos of life's everyday materialism focuses us on the shortest term, on immediate comparisons and competition. Thus we must make conscious efforts to keep the longer-term purpose and the eternal spirit in focus, to see beneath the surface and into the soul.

It is not enough to believe; our belief must be implemented.

And even for those who are not quite sure they believe, spiritual application is still the wisest approach to life because it is by living according to certain principles that we often come to know whether they are true. Believing and living are integrated parts of a two-way street. Believing something helps us to live it because we *want* to, and living something helps us to believe it because it works. Each supports and enhances the other. *Things that are true generally work, and things that work are generally true.*

Conscious application of a premortal perspective involves *striving* in day-to-day situations to do three things—each much more difficult than it sounds and vastly more rewarding than one would guess: (1) see yourself spiritually—strive to think of yourself, of your essence, as a spirit who came from a premortal life; (2) see others spiritually—strive to think of others as spirits inhabiting bodies; and (3) see circumstances spiritually—strive to think of what happens to you and around you in a long-term, spiritual perspective.

Seeing Yourself Spiritually

Even if you deeply and thoroughly believe that you have a soul that both predates and postdates earth life, *thinking* of yourself spiritually—being conscious of your soul as your center and your essence—is difficult and requires practice and effort. We are all used to thinking of ourselves physically and mentally. We're thoroughly aware of how our bodies look—of our weight, our physique, our grooming, our dress, every aspect of our appearance. Advertising, in its hundreds of forms, heightens this physical awareness to the point that it threatens to become an obsession. The society around us also conditions us to be highly self-aware, if not self-conscious, mentally and socially. Our self-images are all wrapped up in what we know and who we know.

Your soul, your spirit, the deepest, truest, *longest* part of you is less apparent in a temporal world and thus most likely to be ignored, by others and by yourself.

But you can, with conscious effort, reconfigure your self-awareness and self-perception, *choosing* to think of yourself as an eternal soul, as a spirit who developed your own unique nature and gifts during a premortal existence, as one favored to come to earth in a dramatic and enlightened time, and as a spiritual son or daughter of God who thus has ultimate worth and ultimate potential. This type of spiritual self-regard is much more credible and real than some self-induced form of confidence or esteem. Mental or physical confidence will ebb and flow according to what's happened lately, but spiritual confidence (better called "faith") can be lasting and consistent.

I once heard a deeply thought-provoking speech in which a wise man asked his listeners to consider the vastness of the known universe. He held up a textbook and asked us how thick we thought a book would be if it had as many pages as the number of stars that exist just in the known and named galaxies. (The book he held had over a thousand pages and was about two inches thick.) The answer was, "Thick enough to go around the world 600 times." He reminded us that each page represented a star, and that we were specks on a tiny planet that orbited one of those stars. Just when he had us feeling impossibly humble and small, he ended with one dramatic and paradigm-shifting sentence: "When I look out on the night sky, I see God's handiwork, but when I look out on your faces, I see God's offspring!"

Learning to view yourself spiritually can remove the stress of self-consciousness and competition. It can make you feel more comfortable with yourself and more satisfied in just being yourself.

Once we perceive ourselves spiritually, it becomes more natural to seek spiritual help—to pray and ask for guidance. People in true touch with their spiritual selves can be completely humble, yet remarkably intimate with God. I'll never forget an experience when I had occasion to kneel in prayer with a very wise and elderly man. We were volunteering in a project at the New York World's Fair, and we faced some challenges that he suggested we pray about. We knelt down and he prayed verbally and then suggested that both of us pray silently—individually. While I was doing so, I heard the scratching of a pencil writing rapidly on paper. I assumed he had finished praying and was doing some kind of writing while he waited for me to finish. When I looked up, he was jotting something on a yellow pad but his head was still bowed. He finished, looked up, and said matter-of-factly: "Sometimes if I don't take notes on the answers I get, I tend to forget parts of them." I stared at him, stirred by the realization that, to this spiritual man, prayer was as real as any other form of conversation. He asked, he listened for answers, and he took notes.

Perceiving ourselves spiritually is primarily a matter of concentration and practice, but there are four *related* things we can do that help make it easier:

1. *Respect, Appreciate, and Pay Attention to Your Spirit.* Our spirits furnish us with information all the time—as much as or more than our senses do. Just as you would not ignore the red light that your eyes see or the police siren that your ears hear, do not ignore the impressions or "nudges" that your spirit provides, or the warnings and messages of right and wrong that your conscience sends.

The little intuitions and feelings and promptings that come to our spirits are a bit like radio signals. If we tune them in carefully and pay attention, they become clearer. If we ignore them, they fade into static.

2. *Deny the Physical a Little More.* The more our physical appetites control us, the more physically oriented we become. The more our spirits control our appetites, the more spiritual we become. Try eating less and eating more slowly. Try a twenty-four-hour fast occasionally, seeking the spiritual clarity that can accompany this bridling of appetite. Control other appetites as well: temper, jealousy, sexual impulses. Think of

yourself *as* your spirit, appreciating your body but determining and controlling what it does.

3. *Pray More.* You *are* your spirit when you are praying. We all see God spiritually, so it is natural to see ourselves spiritually when we're praying to Him. Beyond any ritualistic or habitual prayers (blessings on food, congregational prayers in church, and so on), pray personally and spontaneously. Express gratitude to God whenever you are aware of anything He has given you, from a good day to a good sunset. Improve your capacity and ability to ask for what you truly need—for guidance, for faith, for help in making choices, in parenting, in relationships, in strengthening your faith. We become good at praying—at thanking, asking, and receiving—through practice, and in the process, we are constantly reminded of who we are, of our spirit essence.

4. *Spend More Time in Nature.* Whether we're in a vast wilderness or just walking in a park or standing alone in our own garden or even pausing briefly to watch a sunrise, there is a spiritual quality in nature that awakens and makes us more aware of our spirits. Don't be away from nature too long. Try to have some contact every day. Stop your car and get out and

walk through trees. Pause to watch a storm roll in or to observe the colors of a fading sunset. Pick a flower or look closely at a leaf. Be aware of the phases of the moon and the changing length of days. Relate and equate everything in nature with God and with your spirit, for whom it was all created.

Seeing Others Spiritually

We do not see things as they are, we see things as we are" (Anais Nin).

I've always loved that quote because it applies so perfectly in our world. If we're optimistic and positive, we see the world as optimistic and positive. If we're angry or depressed, the world seems that way too. Slightly reworded, the quote also has a deeper spiritual implication:

"When we spiritually see ourselves as we really are, we can spiritually see all other things (and all other people) as they really are."

Seeing other people spiritually—seeing them as eternal spirits, not mere temporary bodies—is the most accurate as well as the most blessed sight we can have. It blesses those we see by giving them complete value and worth in our eyes, and it blesses us by stripping the pride and envy and judgment out of our souls.

When we look at others physically or mentally, it is easy to be aware of their shortcomings . . . and of their superiorities. We see (and judge and compare) their assets and liabilities. We notice the ways in which they are more than we are (and whether we like it or not, we feel traces of envy, or jealousy, or inadequacy). We notice ways in which they're less than we are (and whether we like it or not, we feel traces of pride and condescension). When we view others physically, it's easier to see lust than love, easier to see competition than compassion, easier to see judgment than justice.

When we focus on seeing others spiritually, with our shared premortal existence as the context, everything changes. They are now brothers and sisters, sharing the same eternal goals and participating with us in the same mortal plan and purpose. Instantly, in that perception, our spiritual similarities obliterate our temporal differences.

The first and easiest place to practice the art of seeing others spiritually is with those we love most—our families and our friends. It is a joy-enhancing exercise to "look upon their hearts," to see the eternal nature and goodness of those we love most and to recognize as well the spiritual flaws that they were sent here to overcome. Seeing our children spiritually is both a release of guilt and a reiteration of responsibility. Knowing that who and what they are is largely a matter of who they became in premortal life prevents us from taking too much credit or too much blame. But knowing they entrusted their spirits to our spirits commits us more completely to being the best parents we can be. Seeing friends spiritually allows us to see deeper into their feelings, to know them better, and to help them more.

The second challenge is to see strangers spiritually. The world becomes a different, more interesting, and more beautiful place if we can view fellow passengers on the subway, people in the supermarket, and passers-by on the street as spirit siblings rather than irrelevant, unimportant, unrelated physical strangers. All it takes is practice, and a belief in who they are and where they came from.

The perception of people as spirits from afar is the most fundamental of all paradigm shifts. It affects every interchange or interaction with every person—from those we love most to those we don't even know. I remember sensing this once in the middle of the night after I had gone into the nursery to pick up our fussy, squawking, screaming toddler, who had kept me awake for the past hour. He was dry, he was warm, he'd been fed, he wasn't sick, he had no excuse for his behavior, and I was angry. As I picked him up, though, I thought about his spirit, struggling to adjust to this new earth life, and I realized that, but for order of birth, he could easily have been the dad, snatching me up angrily from my crib. Instantly my feelings were deeper and warmer, and just as quickly he began to settle down. Another day, on a downtown street in Boston on my lunch hour, I was confronted by a shabby, homeless man. He was an interruption and an irritation until I tried to see him spiritually. I took him into a restaurant, bought him lunch, and listened to his story, feeling strongly as it was told that, given different circumstances, it could have been my story.

As with seeing ourselves, seeing others spiritually is largely a matter of effort, concentration, and practice. Once again, though, there are four approaches or "things to concentrate on" that can help:

1. *See into People's Eyes.* The eye really is "the window to the soul." When you make a conscious effort to look into the eyes

of another person, you see and know more about that person than you did before, and you become less conscious of yourself.

As Linda and I sat on the *Oprah* show talking about an earlier book on teaching values to children, we were discussing the value of honesty and candor, and Oprah became particularly interested in the importance of teaching children to look directly into people's eyes. She took a child from the audience and demonstrated with him how much you can see in a person when you look inside through the eyes.

Practice looking into people's eyes, trying to see their feelings, their mood, their state of spirit. Whether it is a glance and a first impression as you look into the eyes of someone you are just meeting or a deeper, longer stare into the eyes of one you love, you can see into the soul through the eyes. And with practice you can learn much through that window . . . about love and longing, about frustration and fear, about interest and intention.

2. *Listen to People's Spirits.* Often it's not people's words but their *tone* that tells you something—not what they say but how they say it. A friend once told me of moving to a different country and trying to learn a new language by just living around the

people. Long before he understood the words, he said, he could understand tones and moods and feelings. He could tell how people were feeling without knowing what they were saying. Since people don't always say what they mean or express what they feel, the words can almost get in the way, obscuring or confusing the real message, which is in the eyes and the voice and the body language. If you try to focus on these things, you begin to hear the spirit.

3. *Take into Account the Spiritual Purpose in People's Situations.* Instead of looking at others judgmentally, look at them with the tolerance and the accommodation of a spiritual perspective. Instead of seeing an overweight person as indulgent and undisciplined or a moody person as rude or insensitive, try to see everyone as a spirit who has been given challenges and tendencies and situations here that were tailor-made to allow growth, expansion, and progress. As you do, others will begin to seem more appealing and attractive to you. Even their little faults will sometimes become endearing, and encouragement will come more naturally to your mind than criticism.

4. *Pray to See Others' Spirits.* Since prayer is spiritual language and the most direct spiritual communication, spending more

time and more effort at it can help you not only to see yourself and God more spiritually but to see the spirit in other people as well. Ask for this perception. Ask for the ability to see into people's spirits through their eyes, to be able to hear their hearts along with their words, to be able to love more and to judge less. And once you have asked, get ready to receive.

Seeing Circumstances Spiritually

Coincidence may be just a word we use when we're unable to see God's purpose. The circumstances and situations of our lives are not pure chance or coincidence, not in the spiritual view. Although much of life seems completely random, it is important to always remember that there is purpose in life and that each of us was put in a particular current of mortality that would bring us into contact with the very people and situations and circumstances that would allow us to fulfill our purpose, to learn what we lacked, and to find the joy we were sent here to gain.

Believe not in a God who meddles in our daily lives or who predestines us to do certain things or end up a certain way. But do believe in a God who loved us in premortal life and who still loves us, who answers prayers, and who puts us in life situations that bring to us the very opportunities we need.

Thinking this way can help us not only to handle crisis and big-time disappointment but to make every day more interesting and more beautiful.

As I've mentioned, my father died when I was fifteen. I was the oldest of five children and tried to help my mother hold the family together. The loss of my dad, to whom I was extremely close, seemed hopelessly random and cruel. Even then, however, I had a belief in a life before life and in a divine purpose and plan. One side of that faith allowed me to continue to feel my father's spirit. The other side gave me the perspective that gradually allowed me to see what I was becoming because of the situation I was in—the responsibility and maturity that were developing within me because of where and who I was.

In day-to-day things there are always little reasons and answers if we look and ask for them. Why did I get stuck in this traffic jam? Why did I get an airline seat by this interesting person? Why did my son wake up and wander into my room in the middle of the night? There is at least the spiritual possibility of an opportunity in everything that happens. A traffic jam might allow your mind to wander to some useful thought that wouldn't have occurred to you otherwise. The person seated next to you might give you an unexpected connection or opportunity (or you might give one to him). You and your son might talk about something important as you tuck him back in bed—something that wouldn't have come up otherwise.

This is not to say that every little incident has some profound purpose, but *life* has a purpose, and many of those little things can tie in to or contribute to that purpose in some small (or occasionally large) way if we look for this and allow it.

Sometimes the currents of purpose are strong enough that we get a second chance to recognize them. A particular person comes into our life, seemingly by chance, for a second or third time, and we begin to feel that he must have some message for us, whether he knows it or not. Or some little thing happens that reminds us of something else that happened. We can train ourselves to pay more attention to coincidence that may not be coincidence.

The important thing to do is to *look* for meaning or possible connections in everything. This can be an interesting pleasure rather than an encumbering pressure. Entertain spiritual possibilities; imagine spiritual potentials. *Wonder* a little about why certain things happen to you and around you. See life as an intriguing puzzle where there is always the possibility of pieces fitting together rather than as a completely chaotic jumble of pure coincidence.

Trying to see things and situations more spiritually (like trying to see yourself and other people spiritually) is a change of perspective that takes time and effort. There are, once again, four approaches that can help:

1. *Cultivate "Spiritual Serendipity."* Serendipity is the ability, through sagacity and awareness, to find something good while seeking something else. A serendipitous attitude is not a passive "wait for good luck to happen" approach. Rather, it involves having goals and plans but being aware of and open to other possibilities so that you notice opportunities and frequently "find something good while seeking something else." Like a horse whose blinders are taken off, we need to see more than the row or furrow in front of us—more than our own narrow little plan. With the blinders off, when something comes up that is not on our to-do list, we see it as an opportunity for an

interesting surprise rather than as an irritation or an interruption. With a serendipity attitude, things that can't be put on a to-do list—a call from an old friend, a sudden need expressed by a child, an exceptional sunset—are noticed and appreciated, even relished. We grow more aware, more sensitive, more flexible. Often our unplanned "serendipities" are spiritual nudges or impressions. As we are responsive to these, the world around us begins to look and feel more spiritual.

2. *Develop "Magnetic" Goals, Sometimes without Plans.* Sometimes our deepest hopes and fondest dreams don't lend themselves to detailed planning. We know we want something, but there is no apparent path to get there. Visualize it, acknowledge it as a goal, and then, realizing that all things are spiritual, *watch* for a way to open up.

3. *Carry the Question "Coincidence or Purpose?" Consciously in Your Mind.* Every time something new or unexpected happens, just entertain the question, "Is there purpose in this?" A chance encounter, something you just happened to notice, the message or meaning of a particular movie or piece of music, a friend of a friend of a friend, some change in your day that you can't control . . . ask, "Could this mean anything?" "Is there a reason

for this?" "What could this lead to?" As you become more spiritually in tune, your spirit will furnish you with answers, and you'll become able to distinguish small happenings of chance from small happenings of destiny.

4. *Pray for Distinguishing Spiritual Discernment.* Ask God for something that logic suggests He would be anxious to give you—this sense of spiritual awareness, recognition, and discernment. Ask to see things as they really are—spiritually. And then be willing to recognize and follow any answers or promptings you receive.

୯ ୯ ୯

You may, in some way, have sensed your own spirit or pondered the possibilities of a spiritual past long before you opened the front cover of this book. Now, as you near the back cover, my hope is that your hope has grown—perhaps into belief. If it has, or when it does, you will begin to see yourself differently and to value yourself more. There will be a similar effect on how you see others, especially your family, and on how you view your circumstances and your life as a whole.

May these differences, as they deepen, direct you toward the Divine.

Postscript: Continuing the Quest

I have tried intentionally not to clutter this book with too many footnotes or cross references. For example, when I mentioned that much of what I believe about life before life came from (and built from) various things I have read, I did not give specific references to each of those readings. Nor did I refer specifically to my own religious convictions beyond my belief in a premortal life. I had two reasons for not doing so.

1. I feel that spiritual fact carries with it its own ring of truth. The spirit within each of us recognizes truth about itself. I wanted your spirit, initially at least, to have a chance to focus directly on the possibility and credibility of what I was saying—not on some series of sources. Beyond being distracting, sometimes sources or labels can prejudice or bias someone negatively or positively. In this book, I wanted you to be able to focus entirely on questions of spiritual possibility, not on questions of temporal credibility.

2. I wanted a reason to hear from you—to stay in touch with those who want to continue the quest. If you'd like to know more of what prompted me to know, e-mail me at rickrick@aros.net or write to me c/o The Fischer Ross Group, 249 East 48th Street, New York, NY 10017.

Reading Group Guide

☙ ☙ ☙ ☙ ☙

Summary

This book explores philosophical and deeply personal questions of the origins of the soul. It is based on the premise that we existed before this life, not in a different incarnation but as ourselves in a different place and type of existence. Suggesting that a belief in a prelife would have a profound effect on how we see ourselves and how we treat others, the author discusses a variety of implications inherent in such a belief. The following questions may serve as a guide to group discussion or personal introspection.

Topics to Consider

1. Do you think it consistent to believe in God but not to believe in a spirit or soul within ourselves? Why or why not?

2. Is where we came from as important a spiritual question as where we are going?

3. To one who believes in a spirit or soul, what are the options or possibilities concerning how that soul began and where it came from?

4. The author lists eleven "questions of this life" on pages 10 and 11. Which of these have you asked yourself? Of the eleven, which do you think are the most important questions?

5. Chapter 2 presents eighteen "prompters" of a life before life (see pages 20–50). What do you think the author does not call them "evidences" or "proofs"? Which of these have you experienced or thought about? Which are most meaningful or compelling to you?

6. In Chapter 3 the author speaks of physical (or sensual) knowing, emotional knowing, and spiritual knowing. Can we know things are true without seeing, hearing, or touching them? What do you think is the most reliable source of knowledge?

7. In balance, do you think it is more "natural" to believe or not to believe in spiritual things? Generally, can you trust your instincts about what "feels right" spiritually?

8. Why do you suppose the author put an "intermission" in this book? What is the purpose of the Kilimanjaro story and experience?

9. Did you notice a change in tone in Chapter 4? What do you think was the author's intent in this change? What does the change have to do with the "intermission"?

10. Was Chapter 4 harder or easier to accept than the first three chapters? Why? What parts of it "rang true" to you as you read? Would you have preferred not to have had the directions and detail of Chapter 4, to conceive of a prelife more generally or more according to your own imagination of it?

11. In Chapter 5, the notion of a prelife is broken into six specific sub-beliefs (see pages 122–23). Which of the six do you find yourself believing? Which are harder to believe?

12. The author then sets forth twenty "benefits" or practical, day-to-day results of believing in a prelife (see pages 123–26). Which of these twenty appeal to you most? Are they

realistic? Is there a direct cause-and-effect connection between these benefits and a belief in life before life?

13. Chapter 6 has been called the "self-help part" of the book. Do you agree with this assessment? Should the author have given suggestions for the "conscious application" of these beliefs, or should those have been left up to the reader?

14. The author, previously known best for his books on family, parenting, and values, says this book is not a departure from his genre. Why do you think he says that? Do you agree?

15. Were you aware of the author's selective use of the pronouns I, *you*, and *we*? What do you think he was trying to portray, and why?